# TIGERS ESSENTIAL

Everything You Need to Know
to Be a Real Fan!

George Cantor

TRIUMPH
B O O K S

Library of Congress Cataloging-in-Publication Data

Cantor, George, 1941–.
    Tigers essential : everything you need to know to be a real fan! / George Cantor.
        p. cm.
    Includes bibliographical references.
    ISBN-13: 978-1-57243-941-2 (hard cover)
    ISBN-10: 1-57243-941-6  (hard cover)
    1. Detroit Tigers (Baseball team)—History. I. Title.

GV875.D6C36 2006
796.357'640977434—dc22

                                                        2006031651

This book is available in quantity at special discounts for your group or organization. For further information, contact:

**Triumph Books**
542 South Dearborn Street
Suite 750
Chicago, Illinois 60605
(312) 939-3330
Fax (312) 663-3557

Printed in U.S.A.
ISBN: 978-1-57243-941-2
Design by Patricia Frey
All photos courtesy of AP/Wide World Photos except where otherwise indicated

To my mother:
a Tigers fan by osmosis

# Contents

# Introduction

The statues tell the story.

They are lined up in a row in the pavilion behind dead center field at Comerica Park.

Ty Cobb. Charlie Gehringer. Hank Greenberg. Hal Newhouser. Al Kaline. Willie Horton.

They represent an unbroken line of 72 years. Between 1905 and 1977, there was not a single season in which at least one of these men did not play for the Detroit Tigers. And if they ever decide to put Alan Trammell's statue out there, too, the string would be extended to 1996.

This is a continuity almost unprecedented in professional sports, and one of the big reasons this team and this city are so closely connected. There was a constant star, always someone who had been with the Tigers so long that it almost seemed he was part of the texture of Detroit.

But it is much more than that. Because, in reality, the team and the town grew up together.

When the Tigers played their first American League season, in 1901, Detroit was a medium-sized midwestern city known for making stoves and railroad carriages. Within a decade, however, the new automobile industry would turn the city into the United States' economic dynamo, and the rip-roaring Tigers of Cobb would terrorize the rest of the league.

People came here from all over North America and Europe to build the cars. Many could not even speak English. But the Tigers gave them something in common, something to cheer for.

When Detroit was ravaged by the Great Depression, it was the Tigers of Gehringer and Greenberg who taught a defeated city how to hope again.

As World War II transformed the city's industrial might into the Arsenal of Democracy, it was the Tigers of Newhouser who supplied the right note of celebration, winning the World Series just two months after the return of peace.

When Detroit was shaken to its core by the deadly riots of 1967, it was the Tigers of Kaline and Horton who helped to heal a frightened community.

And in the face of decline, with the automotive industry buffeted by foreign competition and the city bleeding population to the suburbs, it was the Tigers of 1984 who gave its people an identity to be proud of. Even today, say "35 and 5" to anyone in Michigan and they will know immediately what it means: that team's unbelievable season-starting streak.

This history has made the stylized Old English *D* that appears on the caps and home uniforms of the Tigers one of the most recognizable emblems in the sports world.

Elden Auker, who pitched for the 1935 champions, spoke movingly 64 years later at the closing ceremonies for Tiger Stadium. He talked about what it felt like to wear that *D* on your chest and how it defined you for the rest of your life. "Once a Tiger, always a Tiger," he said.

That's why those who carped at the inclusion of Horton in that row of statues at Comerica Park were so wrongheaded. The other five statues do, in fact, celebrate players who were elected to Cooperstown. Willie was not, and, in all likelihood, never will be.

But he represented something more. He was one of millions of kids who grew up in Detroit and could dream of nothing greater than to walk onto the diamond wearing that uniform. That dream came true for him, and for more than a decade his towering home runs thrilled Tigers fans who saw him as one of their own.

For those of us who had to give up that dream for others which were far less exalted, Willie stands for the good seasons, the thrilling memories, and the power of a history shared—and the wonders still to come, as the Tigers rise again and we go through the years with our city and our team.

# Charlie Bennett's Ballpark

It wasn't much, even by the undemanding standards of 1901. There were only 8,500 seats, the smallest ballpark in the major leagues. The playing field was laid out over an old hay market that had been paved with cobblestones, and infielders knew that batted balls could take some absolutely remarkable bounces. There was just one tiny clubhouse, so visiting teams had to change clothes at their hotels. Showers? Be serious.

Still, the opening of Bennett Park was cause for celebration in Detroit, and by popular acclamation it had been named for the city's greatest baseball hero, Charlie Bennett.

In his day Bennett had been a fine catcher. More than that, he was a link to the most glorious chapter in the city's baseball history: the world championship of 1887. But seven years later, playing with Boston, he had been involved in a terrible accident. While his train was stopped at a small town, Bennett jumped off to visit some friends. When he tried to reboard, he lost his balance and fell beneath the wheels. Both legs were crushed and had to be amputated.

With his career finished, Bennett returned to Detroit and opened a cigar store. But the city never forgot him. Now, in 1901, big-league baseball had come back to town at last, and in the ballpark that bore his name.

When Charlie made his way to home plate to catch the ceremonial first pitch of Detroit's American League opener, strong men in derby hats wept without shame. It had been a tough struggle to reach this moment. Detroit was not a popular choice to get a franchise in the new league. Cleveland was dead set against it, and a few

1

**.299**—Detroit's team batting average in 1887, 20 points higher than any other team in the National League.

other club owners were highly dubious. They wanted to go into Pittsburgh instead, and bang heads with the Pirates.

But Ban Johnson felt differently, and as the president and driving force behind the new league, his word trumped all opposing arguments. Besides, the owner of the Detroit team was also the county sheriff. Didn't that count for something?

So it was almost by imperial fiat that the Detroit Tigers became a charter member of the American League.

They had been called the Tigers for about six years. The nickname first appeared in local newspaper headlines and referred to the stripes on the uniform sleeves of the Detroit team in the Western League. This was the minor league that Johnson was trying, against all odds, to levitate into a second major league.

Besides the less than splendid ballpark, moreover, the city had a history with major league baseball, and it wasn't a promising one.

The Detroit Wolverines had joined the National League in 1881 and for five years was one of its more nondescript members. But after the 1885 season, the team's owners bought the entire Buffalo franchise and transferred four of its starters to Detroit. By this simple expedient, the Wolverines were turned into an instant contender. It also brought down the wrath of all the other owners, who didn't like the idea of throwing money around like that. After all, it might give the players funny ideas about salaries.

The Wolverines grappled with the world champion Chicagos for most of 1886. Special trains were put on between the cities, so delirious Detroit fans could follow their new heroes. They eventually lost the pennant by 2½ games, but in 1887 they came back in unstoppable fashion.

With a lineup full of sluggers, anchored by Big Dan Brouthers (one of the Buffalo transfers) and Big Sam Thompson, who led the league in hitting, Detroit cruised to its first pennant. Both of these "Big" guys, by the way, stood 6'2" and weighed 207 pounds, according to *The Baseball Encyclopedia*. They would barely qualify as Average

Dan and Sam in today's supersized sports environment. But they were giants in their times and both would go on to the Hall of Fame.

The team went on to defeat the St. Louis Browns of the American Association for the world championship. It was the longest such series in history, with Detroit coming out ahead, 10 games to five. A traveling roadshow, with games scheduled in a number of different cities in front of fans who couldn't have cared less, the series simply dribbled to an end when the customers stopped showing up.

Next year it all fell apart. The team slumped, attendance plummeted, the manager was fired, cash flow dried up, and the other owners were in no mood to bail out this reckless franchise.

Just two years after becoming champions of the world, the Wolverines were gone. The franchise was disbanded, its stars scattered to other teams, and Detroit's run in the majors was finished.

Charlie Bennett had been there for the entire run. In the early going, he was probably Detroit's best player. A smooth receiver at a

*Bennett Park was the Tigers' first home in the American League, named for Charlie Bennett, star catcher for Detroit's championship team in the National League in the 1880s. After the park was reconfigured in 1912, it became Navin Field.*

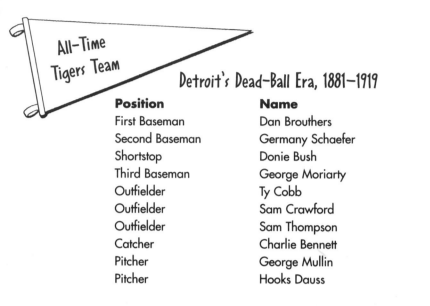

All-Time Tigers Team

**Detroit's Dead-Ball Era, 1881–1919**

| Position | Name |
|---|---|
| First Baseman | Dan Brouthers |
| Second Baseman | Germany Schaefer |
| Shortstop | Donie Bush |
| Third Baseman | George Moriarty |
| Outfielder | Ty Cobb |
| Outfielder | Sam Crawford |
| Outfielder | Sam Thompson |
| Catcher | Charlie Bennett |
| Pitcher | George Mullin |
| Pitcher | Hooks Dauss |

position that was far more prone to bodily harm than it is today, he consistently led all catchers in fielding. He was a solid .300 hitter for a while, too. No wonder the fans remembered him.

There would be other links, too, between the two Detroit franchises. Deacon McGuire, Bennett's backup on the 1885 Wolverines, would return in 1902 to become the starting catcher for the Tigers. Since McGuire's playing career extended over 26 seasons and with 10 different teams, it probably was just a matter of time before he doubled back upon the circuit. Sam Thompson also returned to the Tigers as a coach and got into 31 games as an emergency fill-in at the age of 46 in 1906. But the overall talent on this new team was a bit wan. While other American League franchises had raided the National League for big-name stars, the best the Tigers could come up with was second baseman Kid Gleason from the Giants, pitcher Joe Yeager from Brooklyn, and outfielder Jimmy Barrett from Cincinnati. Along with shortstop Kid Elberfeld ("the Tabasco Kid") and rookie pitcher Roscoe Miller, they gave the team a patina of respectability.

The 1901 opener was encouraging, however. After pregame emotions died, the Tigers were down 13–4 going into the bottom of the ninth. They then scored 10 runs and beat Milwaukee, 14–13, in one of the more remarkable last-ditch rallies in baseball history.

4

The team went on to finish third that year, but in its second season, everything went sour. The hitting was the worst in the league. The remarkable Miller never returned to rookie form and was gone by midseason, with Gleason following soon after. Yeager was so ineffective as a pitcher he was converted to a third baseman. Soon the Tigers dropped all the way to seventh place. The crowds decided to stay away in large numbers—although with just 8,500 seats to sell, the numbers weren't all that large to begin with.

The league's Milwaukee franchise had already been shifted to St. Louis and the Baltimore team was headed for New York. Maybe the original naysayers were right after all and it would have been better to go into established baseball towns instead of dabbling in questionable markets. Would Detroit's franchise be the next one to go?

Charlie Bennett wasn't having any of that. As he would on every Opening Day for the next 23 years, he showed up faithfully at his ballpark to catch the first pitch of the 1903 season.

He had been through the darkest times in life and had been around long enough to know that every new season brings forth fresh promise. You just had to hope for better days.

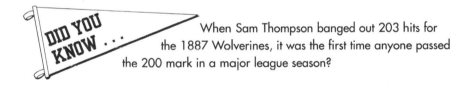

DID YOU KNOW . . . When Sam Thompson banged out 203 hits for the 1887 Wolverines, it was the first time anyone passed the 200 mark in a major league season?

# Wahoo Sam

He never minded the nickname. In fact, he was darn proud of it.

Sam Crawford hailed from Wahoo, Nebraska, and he wanted everyone to know it. He insisted that they put it on his plaque at Cooperstown. Wahoo Sam.

Even in recent years, the name has been a source of fun. David Letterman used Wahoo as the site of his fictitious "home office" for a while on his late night TV show.

But Crawford's memories of his boyhood home, located in the heart of the grain belt, about midway between Omaha and Lincoln, were filled with images of a small-town baseball idyll of the 1890s.

"Every town had its own team in those days," he recalled in an interview shortly before his death in 1968. "We started out in a horse-drawn wagon—the kind they used to haul grain in to the elevators—and 11 or 12 of us fit in and went from town to town playing their teams."

One of the Wahoo boys had a cornet, and when the team arrived in a new town he'd let loose with a blast. People came rushing out to see what was going on, and the team would challenge them to a ballgame.

Crawford loved pointing out that movie executive Darryl Zanuck came from Wahoo, and so did Howard Hanson, a famous classical musician.

It was only when Wahoo Sam arrived in Detroit, in the 1903 season, that the Tigers took their first big step toward becoming big league. He had been a huge star in Cincinnati. In just four years, Crawford established himself as the top slugger in the National

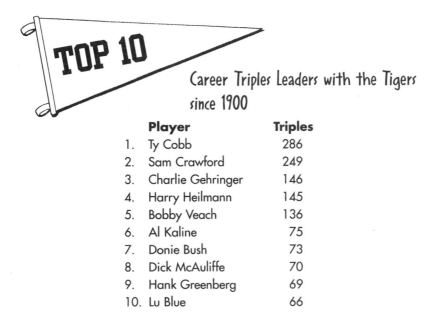

**TOP 10**

Career Triples Leaders with the Tigers since 1900

| | Player | Triples |
|---|---|---|
| 1. | Ty Cobb | 286 |
| 2. | Sam Crawford | 249 |
| 3. | Charlie Gehringer | 146 |
| 4. | Harry Heilmann | 145 |
| 5. | Bobby Veach | 136 |
| 6. | Al Kaline | 75 |
| 7. | Donie Bush | 73 |
| 8. | Dick McAuliffe | 70 |
| 9. | Hank Greenberg | 69 |
| 10. | Lu Blue | 66 |

League. He had led the league in triples and home runs by the time he was 22 years old.

Triples were, in fact, his forte. He hit 309 of them in his career, a mark that will probably never be approached. In the dead-ball era, when clearing the fence was a rarity, a triple was the mark of a true power hitter. "The outfields were a lot bigger in those days," he said by way of explanation for all the three-baggers.

H.G. Salsinger, longtime sports columnist of *The Detroit News*, recalled watching right fielders playing Crawford "right against the fence and catching five fly balls off his bat in one game; five fly balls that would easily have cleared the fence...when the jackrabbit ball was introduced."

Other historians claim that the closest modern equivalent to Crawford in terms of combining power, speed, and defensive skill was Willie Mays. He was that good.

He may have been from Wahoo, but Sam was no hick. He could see the two leagues were coming close to a peace agreement, and the big money that stars were getting for jumping from one to the other was about to dry up. So after the 1902 season he signed with Detroit,

# TRIVIA

This Tigers outfielder of the early 1900s was nicknamed Kangaroo because he jumped between the two major leagues so often. Who was he?

*Answers to the trivia questions are on page 148.*

even though he also had a contract with the Reds.

In a deal reached before the 1903 season, the American League agreed to stay out of Pittsburgh (meaning Detroit was assured of keeping its team), and in the most hotly disputed issue of the meeting, Crawford's contract was awarded to the Tigers. He promptly hit .335, led the league in triples (the first of five times he would do that as a Tiger), and almost single-handedly revived interest in baseball in Detroit.

Crawford would also go on to lead the American League in homers in 1908. He was the only man to win the title in both major leagues until Mark McGwire accomplished it exactly 90 years later. When he retired, in 1917, he held the league's career record for home runs with a grand total of 70—or the same number McGwire hit in one big season in 1998.

Crawford had trained as a barber back in Wahoo. He didn't like it much. Cleaning out the spittoons, mopping hair off the floor, practicing his haircuts on the occasional tramp who came through town and volunteered to sit in his chair for free.

"Saturdays were the worst," he said, "because that's when all the farmers came to town for a shave and a haircut. We were on our feet from 7:00 in the morning to 10:00 or 11:00 at night. After a few days like that, baseball looked pretty good to me.

"That's when I started touring Nebraska with the Wahoo team in the farm wagon. I was 18 years old. A scout saw me and the next year I signed to play with Grand Rapids in the Western League. They sold my contract to Cincinnati in 1899. I was making $150 a month, which was a lot of money in those days. At least for me it was. It all happened in less than two years."

Crawford usually played right field because of the strength of his throwing arm, but he had the speed to play center when that was required. Even-tempered and friendly, he was a manager's dream.

The Tigers had some good ones, too, in those first years. George Stallings, who led the club in its first year, would go on to take the

1914 "Miracle Braves" to a championship. Ed Barrow, Detroit's manager in Crawford's first two seasons, would win the 1918 World Series with the Red Sox and then turn the Yankees into a dynasty as a front-office executive.

The trouble was the other players on the field did not match up to Crawford. He was far and away the best hitter on the Tigers, and for a few seasons the only real threat. Opponents soon learned to pitch around him and deal with the rest of the soft lineup.

"We had some real pitchers back then, too," he said. "It seems we were facing Ed Walsh every other day. We saw Walter Johnson in his first game. I hit a home run off him, too. Walter always liked me

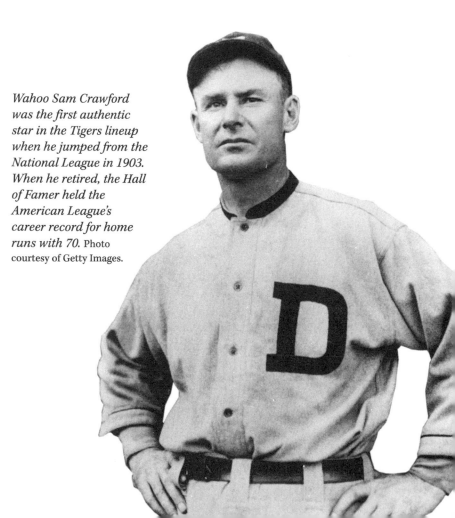

*Wahoo Sam Crawford was the first authentic star in the Tigers lineup when he jumped from the National League in 1903. When he retired, the Hall of Famer held the American League's career record for home runs with 70.* Photo courtesy of Getty Images.

because he wanted to use my bats. Rube Waddell. Oh, my goodness. If he wasn't so easy to distract he might have been the best ever."

One Hall of Famer who neglected to pitch around Crawford, to his regret, was Cy Young. Wahoo Sam's single off him in a 1904 game broke Young's streak of 24⅓ consecutive hitless innings, still a record. (An extra-inning game and a relief appearance figured in there, too.)

Detroit continued to founder in the second division for most of Crawford's first years with the club. But now there was a foundation.

# Along Came Cobb

He swept through baseball like a typhoon; a force that turned a game into psychological, and physical, warfare.

Professional baseball in 1905 was no place for shrinking violets. Rough characters filled its dugouts. When a gentleman athlete, such as Christy Mathewson of the Giants, achieved success it was regarded as remarkable.

But the sport had never seen anything like the fury of Tyrus Raymond Cobb.

Before the emergence of Babe Ruth and the home-run ball in the 1920s, Cobb was the game's unchallenged paradigm. The greatest hitter ever. The most skilled base runner. A plaque that adorned the outer wall of Tiger Stadium for many years called him "a genius in spikes."

Both nouns are important. He was truly a genius at extracting the last ounce of ability he possessed to defeat the opposition. But he was not shy about using whatever weapons were available to him—including his spikes on any infielder who dared get in his way. He would just as soon shred their legs to ribbons as look at them, and they all knew it. As a result, the Tigers of Cobb were the most feared and hated team in baseball for most of two decades.

Author and critic John K. Hutchens described what it was like watching Cobb play in Chicago. When he "stretched a double into a triple, coming into third with his fall-away hook slide, he generated an excitement—a wrathful excitement, to be sure, on the part of White Sox fans—the like of which I have never known in a ballpark. If he then stole home, and there was always the unnerving chance that he would try to, the game and the crowd came apart at the seams."

Cobb's fights were legendary. He fought Buck Herzog of the Giants over a meaningless spring exhibition game. He fought his minor league roommate, Nap Rucker, over who could use the bathroom first. He went into the stands in New York to beat up a heckler, who turned out to be a paraplegic. Even mild-mannered Connie Mack called him "the dirtiest player ever."

He fought his own teammates. Sam Crawford, who didn't much care for him, said that the Georgia-born Cobb acted as if he was still "fighting the Civil War and we were all damn Yankees." Even years later, Crawford refused to say that Cobb was the greatest player he had ever seen, giving that accolade to Honus Wagner instead.

Hall of Famer Charlie Gehringer said Cobb suddenly stopped speaking to him in his rookie year and never told him why. Tigers catcher Boss Schmidt was a hero to his teammates because he once beat up Cobb in a fistfight.

"He antagonized so many people that hardly anyone would speak to him, even among his own teammates," said Davy Jones, who played center field between Cobb and Crawford. "He had such a rotten disposition that it was damn hard to be his friend. And I was probably the best friend he had on the club."

But from the moment he joined the team, halfway through the 1905 season, Cobb became the Detroit Tigers in the minds of their fans. He also became rich by investing in Detroit's infant automotive industry—and in Coca Cola back home in Georgia.

Entire books have been written trying to analyze Cobb's psychological makeup. What makes a man treat his life like an unending battleground? Most historians claim it went back to the death of his father, a respected judge, who was shot to death in his own home by his wife. She claimed she thought he was an intruder who had broken in. Cobb adored his father, and there were rumors that his mother had been involved with another man. He was then 18 years old, already a minor league star at Augusta and just 10 days away from joining the Tigers. Those who knew him said that he was never the same person afterward.

# TRIVIA

The Tigers have retired five uniform numbers, but not Ty Cobb's. How come?

*Answers to the trivia questions are on page 148.*

*This is how Ty Cobb terrorized Detroit's opponents for more than 20 seasons—with spikes high in a billowing cloud of dust. Here he is sliding into third base against Philadelphia.*

Back in those days, stories by local journalists could persuade major league teams to scout a prospect. Grantland Rice, who would become the best-known sportswriter in America but was then a young reporter in Nashville, glowingly described the feats of Cobb for his paper. The Tigers decided to take a look and offered him a contract.

Rice had been tipped to Cobb's ability by letters from an anonymous Augusta fan. Almost 50 years later, Cobb confessed to Rice that he had written the letters himself. He already knew all about getting an edge.

Cobb claimed that he resented the way the Tigers greeted him as a rookie, and that it fueled much of the antagonistic attitude. Crawford waved that off.

# TOP 10

## Tigers with Most Stolen Bases in a Season

| | Player | SB | Year |
|---|---|---|---|
| 1. | Ty Cobb | 96 | 1915 |
| 2. | Ty Cobb | 83 | 1911 |
| 3. | Ron LeFlore | 78 | 1979 |
| 4. | Ty Cobb | 76 | 1909 |
| 5. | Brian Hunter | 74 | 1997 |
| 6. | Ty Cobb | 68 t | 1916 |
| | Ron LeFlore | 68 t | 1978 |
| 8. | Ty Cobb | 65 | 1910 |
| 9. | Ty Cobb | 61 | 1912 |
| 10. | Ron LeFlore | 58 | 1976 |

"We weren't cannibals or heathens," he said. "All rookies got a little hazing. Cobb took it the wrong way. But it was his persecution complex that made him great."

Cobb would sit in the Detroit dugout sharpening his spikes, in full view of the other team's infield practice. He would wear weights in his regular shoes so that when he put on his spikes it made him seem faster.

When National League president Harry Pulliam saw him play in the 1908 World Series, he said, "That young man isn't reckless, as we were told. He's one of the wonders of baseball."

By his second season with the Tigers, Cobb was their leading hitter, despite being sidelined for two months with a hip injury caused by too many slides on the rock-hard infield of Bennett Park. In 1907 he led the league in hitting. His .350 mark was 103 points higher than the league average, and 27 points higher than the runner-up, Crawford. In 1909 he was 133 points above the league average. That's a fair gauge of how dominant he was in his time.

Cobb and Crawford combined to lead Detroit to three straight pennants, from 1907 to 1909. Cobb would lead the league in hitting for nine straight years and 12 of the next 13. In two of those years, he hit over .400, and he did it again in 1922, only to finish second to

George Sisler. His record of 96 stolen bases in 1915 stood for 47 years, until Maury Wills broke it. Cobb's mark for hits in a career, 4,191, was surpassed by Pete Rose. In fact, most of the records he once held have fallen.

Only that lifetime batting average of .367 has never been touched. At the age of 41 he could still hit .323 for the Philadelphia A's, although many of his teammates said that his defensive lapses cost them the pennant. Even then nobody liked him much.

After the three straight pennants at his career's beginning, and three straight failures in the World Series, he never got another chance at a championship. For that reason, a few critics have denigrated his achievements, saying that he came up short in the only category that really matters.

That's a sentimental way of looking at it, though. Most baseball men, then and now, will say that what really really matters is the bottom line.

By becoming the greatest gate attraction the game had ever seen, Cobb turned the shaky Detroit franchise into one of the most solid in baseball and filled ballparks across the league. The crowds always went away knowing they had seen the game played like they had never seen it before.

In 1925 he even hit three home runs in one game, at Sportsman's Park in St. Louis. He was convinced that the home-run addiction created by Babe Ruth had destroyed the game he loved, and he hated it. Most people thought he swung for the fences that day just to show his contempt, and to prove if he really wanted to, he could play it that way, too.

By the NUMBERS **.377, 9 home runs, 107 RBIs**—Cobb's stats when he won the Triple Crown in 1909, the only time a member of the Tigers has done it.

# Eee-Yah

If ever a man was born to manage the Tigers of Ty Cobb, it was Hughie Jennings. He had played shortstop on the Old Orioles and learned his baseball in the hell-for-leather, bend-the-rules, take-no-prisoners style of the great Baltimore teams of the 1890s. He still holds the career record for being hit by pitches, and earned that honor by wearing out-sized uniforms that would get brushed by anything thrown inside. Once he was beaned and lay unconscious in a hospital for three days. But you just shook off that sort of thing with the Orioles.

His best friend was John McGraw, and Jennings brought the same brand of ferocity to the Detroit dugout.

The red-haired, freckle-faced Jennings was an educated man. He earned a law degree from Cornell University, maintained a legal practice in the off-season, and was known as an eloquent trial attorney. He also invested profitably in real estate and banks.

But standing in the third-base coach's box, pawing the ground with his spikes and yelling "Eee-yah" to incite his team and whip the fans into a frenzy, Jennings was the very image of rowdy defiance. He explained later that his distinctive yell was meant to be a shortened version of "Here we are."

Once he even used a tin whistle to raise the noise level and was suspended 10 days for violating the rules. The Old Orioles never cared much for rules.

By the end of the 1906 season, the Tigers recognized what they had in Cobb. They also knew they needed a manager who could direct his talent and rouse the rest of the team to the pitch of its young star. They found their man in Jennings, who was then managing Baltimore's Eastern League team.

**IF ONLY . . .** Catcher Charlie Schmidt had held on to a game-ending strikeout in the ninth inning of Game 1 in the 1907 Series. Instead, the tying run scored on his passed ball, the game ended in a tie, and the Tigers never won again.

In just one year he took the Tigers from sixth place to the World Series. Then he did it twice more. The end result, however, was that Detroit became the only American League team to lose three Series in a row.

The Tigers were more than merely Cobb. Sam Crawford was at the peak of his Hall of Fame career. George Mullin and Wild Bill Donovan were established pitchers. Claude Rossman was a decent first baseman. But it was Cobb who made them more than the sum of their parts.

Jennings saw a kindred spirit in his young star and was willing to give Cobb his head...on the field. "Do what you think is necessary and I'll back you up," Jennings told him.

But Cobb's uncontrollable outbursts of temper off the diamond, his fights, his outspoken racism, and the palpable dislike his teammates felt for him bothered the manager. There were reports that Jennings wanted to trade him to Cleveland for outfielder Elmer Flick. Fortunately, the deal fell through.

Although the Tigers were the class of the American League, they were no match for the Chicago Cubs in the World Series. In 1907 and 1908, they won a total of just one game.

Ban Johnson, the American League president, blamed mixed loyalties. "We do all right in the World Series until that damn National Leaguer Jennings gets into it," he said. "Then we get the hell beaten out of us."

In reality, Jennings was urged on by his old pal McGraw to take revenge for him in the 1908 Series. The Giants manager believed the Cubs had stolen the pennant from him in the infamous Fred Merkle "bonehead" play. But the Tigers could not begin to stop the Chicago machine.

White Sox catcher Billy Sullivan, who had gone up against the Cubs and beaten them in the 1906 Series, predicted what would happen. He said the Cubs would run on Detroit's catcher, Charlie

By the
NUMBERS
**6,210**—The attendance at Bennett Park for the fifth and final game of the 1908 Series. It remains the smallest World Series crowd in history.

Schmidt. Sullivan was on target. The Cubs ran amok, stealing 18 bases in 1907 and 15 more the following year—still the two highest totals ever in a five-game Series.

After a lackluster Series in his first appearance, Cobb hit .368 in the second one and dazzled the Cubs with his base running. But to no avail.

It did, however, set up the most highly anticipated Series up to this time. In 1909 the Tigers met the Pittsburgh Pirates, and that meant Cobb was matched against Honus Wagner. They were the two greatest hitters in the game. Cobb had won three batting titles in a row and Wagner four. Wagner was loved by fans and admired by other players, Cobb universally despised.

It was youth versus experience, good versus evil. ESPN couldn't have scripted it any better.

As far as most of the country was concerned, experience and good won out. Wagner outhit Cobb by 98 points, .333 to .231. He also split Cobb's lip open by tagging him on the mouth in an attempted steal of second.

Jennings was a shrewd operator. He knew he could not return to the Series with the same team that had been chewed up by the Cubs. During the course of the 1909 season he remade his entire infield. He traded for veterans Jim Delahanty, George Moriarty, and Tom Jones, and installed rookie Donie Bush at shortstop. It was a brilliant job of managing and enough to edge out the Athletics by 3½ games.

Unfortunately, Jennings stubbornly stood by his catcher, Schmidt, and the results were awful again. The Pirates stole 18 times on him, another Series record. That ended Schmidt's days as a regular catcher—albeit too late for Detroit.

It was a brutal Series, the first to go the distance in a seven-game format. The Tigers pulled even in Game 6, with a ninth inning that would go down as one of the wildest in history. There were two separate brawls, one after Jones was knocked unconscious on a play at first base and another when Schmidt was spiked on a play at the plate. Moriarty also had to leave the game when he was spiked on a play at third. Managers and players repeatedly left the dugout, snarled curses at each other, and had to be pulled apart by umpires and league officials.

The Tigers won, but half of their reconstituted infield went down with injuries. In the Series finale, rookie Babe Adams beat Detroit for the third time, 8–0.

Jennings was crushed. While he would remain with the Tigers for 11 more seasons and got close once or twice, he never managed in the Series again. It was also Cobb's last Series appearance, and in later years he would say that he wished he had appreciated the opportunity more when he was younger.

The two men grew to be close friends in adversity. But the frustration of defeat gnawed at the manager and he developed a drinking problem before finally turning in his resignation after the 1920 season.

The man who succeeded him was Cobb.

# Navin Field

The high-flying Tigers had outgrown tiny Bennett Park. That much was obvious. After three straight pennants, and with the greatest gate attraction in baseball in their lineup, they had doubled attendance figures of the early years and were closing in on half a million admissions a year.

Frank Navin knew in his bookkeeper's soul now was the time to grow.

He had been hired in 1902 to oversee the team's finances. But as the years went by, and the owners themselves showed little interest in baseball, Navin slowly expanded his role. He bought a 10 percent stake and was eventually named president of the Tigers. By the end of 1909, his minority stake had made Navin a rich man; wealthy enough to buy the team outright. The first order of business in his mind was replacing the outmoded ballpark.

Everyone was doing it. Baseball was in the midst of the greatest expansion in its history. In the next five years, nine ballparks were built. Navin's would outlast all except Boston's Fenway.

He liked the location of Bennett Park, just west of downtown, at Michigan and Trumbull, so he decided to stay put and expand the seating to 22,000. To make room for the expansion, home plate was relocated to where right field used to be. Incredibly, all the construction was completed in just one off-season.

The opening of this park, in April 1912, is accepted as the true birth date of the facility that would become Briggs and then Tiger Stadium. Although Navin protested mildly, it was decided to call the facility Navin Field.

*Out come the fruit and vegetables from the left-field stands after the Cards'
Ducky Medwick spiked Detroit's Marv Owen in Game 7 of the 1934 World
Series. Commissioner Kenesaw Landis had to remove Medwick from the
game.*

**TOP 10**

## Tigers Career Wins by a Pitcher

| Player | Years | Wins |
| --- | --- | --- |
| 1. Hooks Dauss | 1912–26 | 221 |
| 2. George Mullin | 1902–13 | 209 |
| 3. Mickey Lolich | 1963–75 | 207 |
| 4. Hal Newhouser | 1939–53 | 200 |
| 5. Jack Morris | 1977–90 | 198 |
| 6. Tommy Bridges | 1930–46 | 194 |
| 7. Dizzy Trout | 1939–52 | 161 |
| 8. Bill Donovan | 1903–12 | 141 |
| 9. Earl Whitehill | 1923–32 | 133 |
| 10. Frank Lary | 1954–64 | 123 |

Navin was not fast with a dollar and his salary fights with Ty Cobb became the stuff of legend. By the end of his career, Cobb was independently wealthy but still insisted on going to the mat with Navin over every contract.

In one legendary encounter, Navin agreed to pay his star $50,000. But he called Cobb back and told him that Ban Johnson only made $40,000 as American League president. How would it look? So why not accept 40 grand and he'd tack on another 10 grand as a "bonus." Cobb reluctantly agreed.

A few days later, at a banquet in Cobb's honor, Navin got up and said the player had meant so much to Detroit that out of sheer gratitude he was presenting him with a check for $10,000. Even Cobb had to admire his gall.

It also gratified Navin that the realignment of the ballpark allowed him to tear down a row of apartment buildings that stood behind the former left-field wall. The team had hung sheets behind the stands to block the view, but that never seemed to get the job done entirely. Navin was still the keeper of the books and didn't like giving away the product for free.

But he was also that rare owner who knew baseball. He stayed on top of every personnel move, consulting with manager Hughie

Jennings frequently, trying to find the combination that would drive the Tigers to the top again.

In this quest, he would suffer through 25 years of disappointment. Always one of the top hitting teams in the league, Detroit never could muster quite enough pitching to break through. The jackrabbit ball replaced the dead ball, and it was still the same story. He even traded away 26-year-old batting champion Heinie Manush, a future Hall of Famer, to try to get the help he needed.

Maybe it was the manager. He named one of his favorite players, George Moriarty, to succeed Cobb in that job. Then he engineered a deal with Washington to bring their manager, Bucky Harris, "the Boy Wonder," to the Tigers.

Nothing seemed to work until he pried Mickey Cochrane from the debt-ridden Philadelphia A's for $100,000 and made the catcher his manager in 1934. It was a staggering amount of money in the Great Depression, but Navin figured he could double his attendance with a contender and make it up. He won that bet.

He was no stranger to making a wager. Navin's penurious habits did not extend to the ponies. Conservative in every other area of his life, and sought out by other owners for advice on baseball finances, Navin had a weakness for betting on racehorses. It was widely reported that his personal finances were shaky because of investments in his own stable. Although baseball commissioner Kenesaw Landis disapproved, he thought too much of Navin's integrity to interfere.

Besides, the Tigers always were a good show, even in the lean years.

There was Moriarty, whose specialty was stealing home. He did it 11 times in one season and became the subject of an inspirational editorial in *The Detroit News*. "Don't Die on Third" was reprinted millions of time, handed out in pamphlet form by the Ford Motor Company, and recited at countless sales meetings. The article made Moriarty a national figure. It exhorted young men who had reached the threshold of success through their own abilities and the sacrifice of parents to take up the dare and make the final dash to home on their own initiative, just like Moriarty.

There was also shortstop Donie Bush, the best leadoff man imaginable, leading the league in walks four years in a row and setting the

That George Moriarty's grandson, Michael Moriarty, starred in one of Hollywood's best-known baseball movies, *Bang the Drum Slowly*?

table for sluggers Cobb and Sam Crawford. And there was curveball artist, Hooks Dauss, winningest pitcher in Detroit history. And then there was the "Giant Killer," Harry Coveleski. He had beaten the Giants three times in one week as a rookie near the end of the 1908 season. He carried that nickname for the rest of his career, even though he was sent down to the minors shortly thereafter. But after six long years he fought his way back to the bigs with the Tigers and reeled off successive seasons of 22, 22, and 21 wins.

This crew finished the 1915 season with 100 wins, the most ever recorded by the Tigers. Unfortunately, the Red Sox won 101. That was the closest Detroit would come to a flag over the first 25 years of Navin's ownership.

Still, he became a benign and beloved figure in Detroit. For all his tightfisted policies, Navin was a model of civic rectitude in his slightly old-fashioned derby hats and high collars. He was popularly referred to as "Uncle Frank" and regarded as everyone's rich, if slightly eccentric, elderly relative.

Still and all, the quarter-century dry spell bothered him deeply. The old bookkeeper never liked being on the wrong side of the ledger.

# Old Slug

No sport is more enmeshed in the tyranny of numbers than baseball.

Come to bat 10 times and get two hits and you can't play in the big leagues. Get three hits and you may go to Cooperstown.

Consider the case of Harry Heilmann. He is one of the greatest right-handed hitters ever to play the game, which seems to be a bit of a secret. His lifetime average of .342 trails only Rogers Hornsby among the righties since 1900 and is the best in American League history. But while the Rajah was voted into the Hall of Fame as soon as the rules allowed, Heilmann didn't make it until 20 years after his retirement, and one year after his death.

He doesn't even get much respect at home. His statue does not stand with the other Tigers greats in the center-field pavilion of Comerica Park. When fans were asked to vote for the all-time Tigers team in 1999, Heilmann trailed Kirk Gibson for the third outfield slot behind Ty Cobb and Al Kaline.

And it's all because of 11 hits that never happened. Bloops to the infield. Rollers through the infield. Any kind of base hit would have done it.

If he had managed to get four more hits in 1921, five more in 1925, and just two more in 1927, Heilmann would have batted .400 four times. No one has ever done that. If it had happened, he would unquestionably be acknowledged as one of the greatest hitters of all time. Only in 1923, however, did he actually clear the .400 mark. His final averages in those other years—.394, .393, .398.

So very close. The tyranny of numbers.

Those last two titles were won on the last day of the season, incidentally, against pretty formidable competition—Tris Speaker and Al Simmons.

Many of his biographical sketches say that Heilmann was among the slowest players of his time and didn't have the ability to beat out infield hits. Surely, that would have given him the knocks he needed during those three seasons.

But that doesn't quite add up. Even though he played primarily in the hitters' golden era of the 1920s, he still managed to steal 113 bases in his career. That's 82 more than Joe DiMaggio, for example, a player who was never accused of lacking speed.

It also didn't help Heilmann's case that for most of his career he was overshadowed by the man next to him in the Detroit outfield, Ty

*Harry "Slug" Heilmann won four batting crowns during the 1920s, finishing with an average higher than .390 on every occasion. Among right-handers, only Rogers Hornsby had a higher lifetime batting mark.*

Cobb. And he never got to play in the sport's showcase, the World Series.

It was Cobb, however, who showed him how to hit.

Many of those who played for Cobb when he managed the Tigers complained that he was incapable of teaching. "His abilities came to him so naturally," said Charlie Gehringer, "that he couldn't understand why other players couldn't get the same results."

**TRIVIA**

Who is the only man ever to pitch a perfect game against the Tigers?

*Answers to the trivia questions are on page 148.*

Heilmann was the exception. He was a .280 hitter in his first four years with the Tigers. But Cobb took him in hand, placed his feet close together in the batter's box, and concentrated on a stroke that produced sharp line drives; and for the next 12 years Heilmann never went below .300 again.

"It was kind of a choppy swing but powerful," said Ted Lyons, who pitched against him for the White Sox all through the 1920s.

"I hit .334 for the Senators one year," recalled Goose Goslin, "and thought that I was doing pretty good. But I wasn't even within 65 points of Heilmann. To bat .350 when he was around meant nothing."

Heilmann was known as one of the friendliest players in the league. This was something else that didn't sit well with Cobb. The manager took him aside one season and told him to get on another one of the Detroit outfielders, Bobby Veach. Cobb thought Veach needed some goading to get the most out of his talent but didn't want to do it himself. Cobb said that he'd explain to Veach when the season was over.

The plan worked. Veach had a great season, hitting .338 and driving in 128 runs. But Cobb left immediately after the last game and Veach remained furious with Heilmann.

"I went up to him and tried to tell him what happened and Bobby just waved me away, saying, 'Don't come around me now wanting to be my friend,'" said Heilmann. But that's what it was like to play for Cobb.

The Tigers would lead the league in team batting average three times during the '20s and frequently finished hitting over .300. But

By the **NUMBERS** **22**—Batting championships won by Tigers hitters. Ty Cobb, 12; Harry Heilmann, four; one each for Heinie Manush, Charlie Gehringer, George Kell, Al Kaline, Harvey Kuenn, and Norm Cash.

they never came close to a pennant. During the entire decade they produced a grand total of one 20-game-winning pitcher, the aging Hooks Dauss.

"They had so many great hitters on that team that Cobb couldn't even break into the starting lineup...and he was the manager," said Lyons. "Heilmann, Heinie Manush, Fats Fothergill. One right after the other in that lineup. Imagine keeping Ty Cobb on the bench. Fothergill came over to the White Sox later in his career and he'd just laugh and laugh about that."

But the old order was changing in a rush. Cobb went to Philadelphia after the 1926 season, as much a milestone in the city's history as Ford halting production of the Model T the next year. Manush and Fothergill were traded.

In 1929 Heilmann developed arthritis in his hands. Instead of winning another batting title, as he had for every other odd-numbered year in the decade, he "slipped" all the way to .344, with a mere 120 RBIs. Owner Frank Navin took that as a sure sign that he was finished and sold his contract to Cincinnati. Heilmann couldn't compete with the standard he had set for himself.

He continued to make his home in Detroit, though, and after his retirement as a player he became the team's radio announcer, a job he held for almost 20 years.

In 1951, on the eve of the All-Star Game at Briggs Stadium, Heilmann lay dying of cancer in a Detroit-area hospital. Cobb, his old teammate and mentor, paid him a visit. Leaning over his bed, Cobb whispered the news that Heilmann had been elected to the Hall of Fame. The dying man smiled and passed away the next day.

It had been a lie. His overdue election wouldn't come until the next year. But Cobb, always maligned for his lack of compassion, wanted his friend to think that he had made it to Cooperstown before he died.

# Golden Voices

Frank Navin was doubtful. The owner of the Tigers, like most Detroiters, listened to WWJ, the first commercial radio station in the United States. He may even have heard a University of Michigan football game broadcast in 1926 on that station by Ty Tyson.

But when it was proposed that Tyson do play-by-play of all Tigers games on radio, Navin balked. Wouldn't that cut down on the gate? Why should he give away his product? But he reluctantly agreed to sign a contract with a local oil company as a sponsor and try it out on a test basis.

No provision was made for a broadcast booth, so Tyson had to sit in the stands on Opening Day of the 1927 season with a wooden board across his seat to hold his notes. He also had to double as the ballpark's public address announcer.

To Navin's delight and surprise, the broadcasts were a hit. His audience, in fact, expanded. People who hadn't been to a ballgame in years tuned in to Tyson and decided to come out and see what was going on for themselves.

Part of the appeal was Tyson's low-key, dryly humorous delivery. He was a radio pioneer, a staff announcer at WWJ almost from the time it went on the air. He knew radio from the ground up. But he knew baseball, too, and it came across in his broadcasts.

Old timers recall with delight his literary locutions. When relief pitcher Elon "Chief" Hogsett, a Native American, entered a game, for example, Tyson would say, "Here comes the noble red man to take up the white man's burden." While that probably would not pass sensitivity muster today, it was regarded as pretty good stuff in the 1930s.

**IF ONLY . . .** It hadn't rained on July 25, 1967, in Baltimore. The Tigers tried to slow down the city's deadly 1967 riots by hurriedly scheduling TV coverage of a critical game from Baltimore. But it was rained out. The riots lasted four days, and 43 people were killed.

Tyson stayed with it for 15 years, missing just a handful of games until his retirement in 1942. It was said, with little exaggeration, that you could walk down any street in Detroit during the summers of 1934 and 1935 and not miss a pitch. Tyson's voice drifted through open windows from the radio in every home and apartment of those pennant years.

Or the voice could have belonged to former Tigers star Harry Heilmann. Interest in the ballclub was so high that radio station WXYZ hired Heilmann in 1934 to compete with Tyson. The two were friendly competitors until Tyson's retirement, and then Heilmann's station obtained exclusive rights.

Heilmann's home run call—"It's trouble, trouble"—was one of his trademarks, as was the inexhaustible store of tales about his playing days with the Tigers and his insights into the game's nuances. When Heilmann became too ill to work in 1951, Tyson came out of retirement for a season to fill in for his old friend.

The rest of the '50s belonged to the engaging Van Patrick, a bigger-than-life Texan whose radio delivery brought high drama to the fairly pedestrian Tigers teams of that decade. Patrick is best remembered for his longtime association with the Detroit Lions and his calls of their three championship runs in the '50s.

But he knew how to pump up a baseball game, too. When pitcher Billy Hoeft encountered rough waters, Van would intone, "And traffic is slowing down in Oshkosh, Wisconsin." His audience knew that was Hoeft's hometown, but they never thought to ask how Patrick's broadcast was being picked up by motorists way over on the far side of Lake Michigan.

During his tenure in the broadcast booth, Patrick was paired with various former ballplayers, including three years with ex-Tiger Dizzy Trout and three more with Giants great Mel Ott, whose low-key delivery was the perfect antidote to Patrick's histrionics.

Van's run ended after the 1959 season when a new beer sponsor felt he was too closely tied to the old brew. The next year, however, brought in two of the most popular broadcasters in Tigers history.

George Kell had teamed with Patrick during Van's final year. Kell was still a hero in Detroit, where he had won a batting title and played third base at an All-Star level. Kell spoke with a slightly nasal Arkansas twang, and his regionalisms ("He broke his bat half in two") charmed Michigan listeners.

But the Tigers really hit pay dirt in 1960 with the arrival of Ernie Harwell. He would remain for the better part of 42 years, and for two generations of fans he was the heartbeat of baseball in Detroit.

*Ernie Harwell waves good-bye to cheering fans during his last home broadcast, on September 22, 2002. For more than 40 seasons Harwell was the voice of the Tigers and one of the most beloved figures in Detroit.*

Harwell was both reporter and storyteller. He had the ability to describe the action on the field in clear, concise, riveting terms while relating it to other events in the game's storied past. His annual quotation from the Bible's Song of Songs ("The rains are past, the winter is over, and the voice of the turtle is heard in the land") was a welcome sign of the season, the first exhibition game broadcast from Florida. Other Harwellisms—"He stood there like the house by the side of the road," "And that one's looong gone," "A man from Saginaw [or any other Michigan town that happened to come to mind when a foul went into the stands] caught that ball"—were part of the fun of listening to him.

The greatest public relations gaffe in Tigers history was the decision to force him out after the 1991 season. The public outcry was so angry that the men brought in to replace him—Rick Rizzs and Bob Rathbun—never had a chance. They were gone in three years and Harwell was back where he belonged, until his real retirement after the 2002 season. His longest partnership was with Paul Carey, a radio veteran whose deep confident voice sounded like messages from the Almighty.

Kell, for his part, would go on to spend 30 years in the television booth. His most effective pairing was with Al Kaline. These two fine baseball minds would dissect the Tigers' performance in terms that were both understandable to the average fan and, when the occasion demanded, painfully honest.

Since 2003 the team has paired former Detroit utility players on world championship teams with hometown broadcasters. On radio it is Jim Price, backup catcher to Bill Freehan on the 1968 team, and Dan Dickerson. On TV, Rod Allen, who played on the 1984 team, and Mario Impemba, do the job.

It wasn't only broadcasters who built the media image of this team. *Detroit News* sports editor, H.G. Salsinger, was a magisterial figure in Tigers baseball coverage for 50 years—from Ty Cobb to Al Kaline. His column, "The Umpire," was

## TRIVIA

**Which Tiger went straight from the television broadcast booth to become the team's top assistant coach?**

*Answers to the trivia questions are on page 148.*

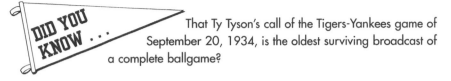

That Ty Tyson's call of the Tigers-Yankees game of September 20, 1934, is the oldest surviving broadcast of a complete ballgame?

regarded as the most authoritative word in town. Even Navin occasionally turned to him for advice on personnel decisions.

Iffy the Dopester was created in 1934 in the pages of the *Detroit Free Press*. Actually a nom de plume for managing editor Malcolm Bingay, Iffy's trenchant observations on the Tigers, written in irreverent and comic slang, became a must-read for local fans and boosted circulation even in the Depression economy.

Joe Falls wrote about the Tigers for both of those papers, plus the defunct *Detroit Times* and the Associated Press, for half a century. His caustic commentaries and ability to come up with the one-liner that would illuminate any given situation ("Rocky Colavito says he wants to play left field. Well, he's got the feet for it") brought him ardent admirers and equally passionate detractors. But he impressed enough people to be voted into the writers' wing at Cooperstown in 2003.

# The Silent Man

They made jokes about him. They called him the Mechanical Man. "You wind him up," said Yankees pitcher Lefty Gomez, "and he hits .333 on Opening Day. When the season ends he's still hitting .333."

They called him the Silent Man, too. In a collection of famous baseball quotes, the one under Gehringer's name read "........."

Gehringer always thought that was a little unfair. True to form, however, he never said much about it.

"I never believed in spouting off to the press and I wasn't one of those holler guys," he said many years after his retirement. "In fact, I think that's what got me in trouble with Ty Cobb when he managed the Tigers in my rookie year. We were playing an exhibition game and he started in on the infielders about not making enough noise. He was looking right at me when he said it, so I said: 'I'm making as much noise as anyone.'

"Well, that did it. He never spoke to me again for most of the season. If he had something to tell me, he'd relay it through a coach. At least, I think that's why he stopped talking to me. He never really explained. Nobody liked him much as a manager. He sure was a peculiar man." Gehringer played second base in Detroit for 16 seasons in a way that defined that position. He was a flawless fielder with a limitless range, and, as Gomez pointed out, one of the most consistent hitters the game has ever seen.

His career batting average was .320. For the three World Series he played in it was .321. And in six All-Star Games, against the best pitchers in baseball, it was .500.

"A bad day for Charlie was a strikeout," said Hank Greenberg. "One strikeout."

"He'd never swing at the first pitch, not even if you lobbed it over the plate," said Wes Ferrell, who faced him many times. "Then you'd get another strike on him and you figured you had him. Then he'd hit that ball and beat you out of a ballgame."

Lefty Grove said he gave him as much trouble as any hitter he ever faced, even though Gehringer swung from the left side.

*They called him the Mechanical Man, and Charlie Gehringer played the game as if it was simply automatic. Flawless in the field, he was one of the most consistent hitters the Tigers ever had.*

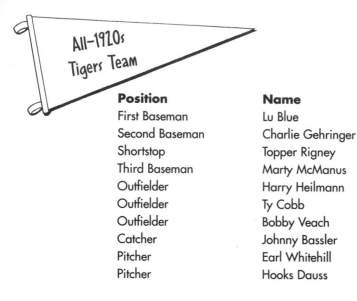

All-1920s
Tigers Team

| Position | Name |
| --- | --- |
| First Baseman | Lu Blue |
| Second Baseman | Charlie Gehringer |
| Shortstop | Topper Rigney |
| Third Baseman | Marty McManus |
| Outfielder | Harry Heilmann |
| Outfielder | Ty Cobb |
| Outfielder | Bobby Veach |
| Catcher | Johnny Bassler |
| Pitcher | Earl Whitehill |
| Pitcher | Hooks Dauss |

In 1936 he played every game, came to bat 641 times, and had just 13 strikeouts. No wonder he never went into a slump. He also hit 60 doubles that year, by the way, and batted .354.

Gehringer was a home-grown hero, which endeared him even more to Tigers fans. He grew up on a farm outside Fowlerville, a rural community on the road from Detroit to the state capital in Lansing. He was discovered by Tigers outfielder Bobby Veach, who used to hunt in the area during the off-season. Veach recommended Gehringer for a tryout, and he came down to Detroit in 1924 to perform before Cobb, Harry Heilmann, and even owner Frank Navin.

"They never said a word but I could feel their eyes watching my every move," said Gehringer. "In fact, after I started fielding grounders at second, Cobb went up to Navin's office in his uniform and spikes and demanded that he come down to watch me. It was eerie. There wasn't another sound in the entire ballpark.

"But they signed me to a contract and in two years I was the regular second baseman."

The Tigers couldn't have known it, but they had just secured the future. A pennant was still eight years away and there would be setbacks before the 25-year drought ended in 1934. But all other moves were built upon the solid foundation of the Mechanical Man.

Gehringer was a bachelor throughout his playing days and lived modestly for several years in a rented room in a private home a few miles from the ballpark. Most of his career was spent during the Depression era, when even Navin was having trouble meeting his payroll and getting the team to spring training. But Gehringer carefully husbanded his resources and when his career ended bought into a successful auto-supply business. Later on he would help rebuild the team as its general manager in the 1950s, carefully crafting the deals that brought it back to respectability after the first last-place finish in its history.

In 1926, though, that was still to come. After Cobb left at the end of that season, George Moriarty was named manager. He had made his reputation for stealing home and was a bit hung up on the subject.

"He had us practicing fadeaway slides in hotel lobbies," said Gehringer. "He thought that was the key to stealing home. We must have set a record that year for getting thrown out on attempted steals of home."

He also had less than fond memories of rooming with slugger Rudy York on the road. The first baseman had a habit of falling asleep with a cigarette in his hand and waking up with the mattress on fire. Gehringer finally had to request a change in roommates as a matter of self-preservation.

"But the Mechanical Man business wasn't that far off the mark," he said. "Much of baseball is a matter of constant repetition, getting it down so that the movements are automatic. At least, that's how I approached fielding.

"That's why an infielder's work is not really appreciated by the average fan. You ask him what's the greatest outfield play you ever saw and he'll come up right away with something by Willie Mays or Joe DiMaggio. Ask about a great play in the infield, though, and he won't have an answer."

He led American League second basemen in defense for six seasons. In 1937, when he also led the league with a .371 batting average, he was voted its Most Valuable Player on a team that finished a distant second to the Yankees.

In the end it was economy and discipline that were essential to Gehringer's success, not only in his personal finances, but also in his

IF ONLY . . . The Tigers had not cut Carl Hubbell from their farm system, then they might have achieved much more. He was cut because Cobb thought Hubbell's screwball was a gimmick pitch. Hubbell went on to win 253 games for the New York Giants.

movements and approach to the game. Do what needs to be done and don't make a big deal about it.

Hitters who were constantly stepping out of the batter's box to go through a little ritual, for example, exasperated him.

"Where do they think they're going?" he asked. "What are they accomplishing? If you go up there to hit, hit. Don't go for a walk."

That's not the way the Mechanical Man would have done it.

# Hammerin' Hank

It was a strange anomaly. The Tigers were near the top of the league in hitting almost every season, but they never had the one hitter they really needed. The long-ball man, the slugger, the home-run king.

Part of this was the fault of Ty Cobb. He despised the home run. He believed in the single, the stolen base, the well-executed hit-and-run. When he managed the team, he sought out players who fit that mold.

But the game had changed. Between 1921 and 1932, the Yankees and Athletics won 10 of 12 pennants with Babe Ruth and Lou Gehrig, Jimmie Foxx and Al Simmons in their lineups. They scored runs in clusters and no lead was safe against them. The Tigers never had that going for them. Before the 1930s, their top home-run hitter in one season was Dale Alexander, who hit 25.

That's why the arrival of Hank Greenberg changed everything. Not right away. He only hit 12 in his first season as a regular in 1933. But the potential was there, and when he did hit his stride the Tigers finally left the dead-ball era behind and began their charge to a pennant.

Greenberg was a big clumsy kid out of New York City. Awkward around first base and slow. But he worked at it. He even took dance lessons to improve his footwork.

"Hank made himself into a great hitter, maybe more than anyone else I ever saw," said Charlie Gehringer. "The same with his fielding. When Rudy York became our first baseman and Hank moved to the outfield, a lot of people thought it would be a disaster. But he did just fine."

"He hit number four in the order, right behind me. All he wanted to do was drive in runs. 'Charlie,' he'd tell me, 'just get 'em to third base. I'll take it from there.'"

His 183 RBIs in 1937 is still a Detroit record for one season.

The other thing about Greenberg is that he was Jewish at a time when anti-Semitism was a major factor in American life. The abuse he took from opposing dugouts and fans was a foretaste of what Jackie Robinson would experience in the following decade.

*When Hank Greenberg came to bat, you couldn't take your eyes off him. With his powerful swing, he was always a threat to put one in the seats. He still holds the Tigers' single-season home-run record of 58.*

IF ONLY . . .  World War II and a hand injury had not interrupted Hank Greenberg's career. In the five seasons immediately before and after his military service, Greenberg averaged 43 home runs a year. Add that to the four war years and the complete season he missed with a hand injury, and he probably would have been close to a 600 career home-run hitter had he played. As it was, he finished with 331.

Robinson said, in fact, that a talk he had with him when Greenberg was playing with Pittsburgh in 1947 stiffened his resolve to take the abuse and go on.

"For some reason, the Yankees were the worst," Greenberg said in later years. "You know, every ethnic group came in for it. Italian, Polish. They'd call you the usual names. The trouble was I was one of the only Jews."

To the Jewish fans of Detroit, Greenberg was the greatest sports hero they had ever known—bigger than Benny Friedman or Harry Newman, who had quarterbacked the University of Michigan to national football titles.

In Germany Adolf Hitler had come to power and already was instituting the policies that would lead to the Holocaust. The "radio priest," Fr. Charles Coughlin, had a nationwide audience for his broadcasts from the suburbs of Detroit in which he inveighed against Jewish financiers.

Every Greenberg home run was a blow against hatred. Even in New York, many Jewish fans of the Yankees prayed silently at their radios that Hank would hit another.

In the midst of the 1934 pennant race, the question of whether he would play during the Jewish High Holidays touched off a theological debate. Some rabbis found references to children playing in the streets of ancient Jerusalem during the Jewish New Year, Rosh Hashanah, and gave him a thumbs-up. But on Yom Kippur, the Day of Atonement, he went to the synagogue instead and became an even greater hero to his fans.

"He's true to his religion, and I honor him for that," wrote poet Eddie Guest approvingly in the *Detroit Free Press*.

## TOP 10

### Career Home Runs for the Tigers

| | Player | Years | HR |
|---|---|---|---|
| 1. | Al Kaline | 1953–74 | 399 |
| 2. | Norm Cash | 1960–74 | 373 |
| 3. | Hank Greenberg | 1933–41, 1945–46 | 306 |
| 4. | Willie Horton | 1963–77 | 262 |
| 5. | Cecil Fielder | 1990–96 | 245 |
| 6. | Lou Whitaker | 1977–95 | 244 |
| 7. | Rudy York | 1937–45 | 239 |
| 8. | Lance Parrish | 1977–86 | 212 |
| 9. | Bill Freehan | 1963–76 | 200 |
| 10. | Kirk Gibson | 1979–87, 1993–95 | 195 |

He hit 26 homers to break the team record that year and upped it to 36 during the championship season of 1935. After an injury-plagued year in 1936, he raised the mark to 40. Then in 1938 he made a run at Babe Ruth's record of 60. At that point, it was less than a decade old and a far less hallowed stat than it was when Roger Maris finally broke it, 23 years later. But Greenberg went through the same bigotry that Henry Aaron experienced when it was his turn to break another of Ruth's treasured home-run records.

Greenberg fell short at 58, hitting none during the season's final week. With the Tigers and their opponents well out of the race, he faced several rookie pitchers who were wild and gave him nothing to hit. In the minds of many fans, however, it was a deliberate policy to keep him from reaching 60.

"The national press had come out to watch Hank break the record," recalled Bob Feller. "So all these cameras were in the ballpark in Cleveland on the last day of the 1938 season when I struck out 18 Tigers and broke the record. That's when I really became a nationally known figure, and I had Hank to thank for it."

Feller struck him out twice that day.

Three years later, even before the United States was at war, Greenberg became one of the first professional athletes to volunteer for military duty. He would miss three complete seasons and most of two others before returning to the big leagues in 1945...right in the middle of another pennant race.

It was still wartime baseball, but the Tigers, the Washington Senators, and the St. Louis Browns were engaged in a classic fight. On the season's final Sunday, the Senators had already finished their schedule, giving up Griffith Stadium to the Redskins. If the Tigers won one game of a doubleheader in St. Louis, they would clinch.

"We were behind in the ninth but put runners on second and third with one out," recalled Detroit center fielder Doc Cramer. "The Browns decided to give me an intentional pass and hoped they could turn a double play on Hank. Instead, he hit it into the bleachers for a grand slam and we won the pennant.

"For years after that, I'd go around telling people, 'You know, they once walked me to get to Greenberg.' And Hank would say, 'Wait a minute, tell 'em the rest of the story.' But I'd always just stop right there."

Why spoil a great line with an explanation?

# Black Mike and Champagne

H.G. Salsinger was not surprised to hear Frank Navin's voice on the other end of the phone. The Tigers' owner frequently consulted with the sports editor of *The Detroit News* as a man whose opinions on baseball he respected.

This time there was an anxious edge in Navin's voice.

"Sal, Connie Mack is offering us Mickey Cochrane for $100,000. I want to name him manager. What do you think? Is he the right man?"

Salsinger didn't hesitate for an instant. "Make the deal," he said.

It was two weeks before Christmas, 1933, and the Tigers had been given an early present: the next two American League pennants.

Mack had assembled one of the greatest teams in baseball history in Philadelphia. All-Stars everywhere you looked. Jimmie Foxx, Al Simmons, Lefty Grove, Moose Earnshaw, Jimmie Dykes. But its soul was Cochrane.

But the team was on the downswing and the Depression was strangling the Athletics. It was time to unload them for cold cash in order to survive.

Cochrane had slipped a bit in 1933, mirroring the team's fall to third place, 19½ games behind Washington. But he was still a .300 hitter and caught 128 games. And he had the passion. It was Cochrane's blazing will to win that had sparked those teams to three pennants and two World Series rings.

Nicknamed Black Mike, he was a brooding Boston Irishman. The finest catcher of his times. He handled pitchers masterfully and played flawless defense.

*The fiery leader of the 1934–35 pennant winners, Mickey Cochrane defied other teams to beat him. As player/manager he inspired a Depression-ridden city and brought Detroit its first world championship.*

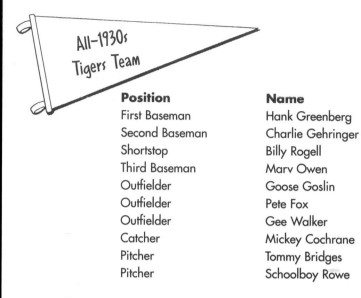

**All-1930s Tigers Team**

| Position | Name |
|---|---|
| First Baseman | Hank Greenberg |
| Second Baseman | Charlie Gehringer |
| Shortstop | Billy Rogell |
| Third Baseman | Marv Owen |
| Outfielder | Goose Goslin |
| Outfielder | Pete Fox |
| Outfielder | Gee Walker |
| Catcher | Mickey Cochrane |
| Pitcher | Tommy Bridges |
| Pitcher | Schoolboy Rowe |

"All the years he caught me I don't think I shook off a sign more than five or six times," said Grove. "I'd look up for the sign and he was calling for the pitch I already had in my mind to throw. That's the kind of catcher he was."

"You didn't want to get too close to him in the clubhouse after a 1–0 loss," added Doc Cramer, who broke in with those teams.

But could the fire within him catch a spark on a team he managed? After all, Cobb also was a man who had treated each loss like a little death. As a manager he had been a bust and Bucky Harris was brought in to try the calmer approach. Now he, too, was out, and it was back to passion.

For all their promise, the Tigers were a lackluster fifth-place team in 1933. More to the point, attendance had plummeted to 321,000—the lowest in Navin Field history aside from the war year of 1918. There had been no pennant in 25 years. Ty Cobb was long gone. People had other uses for their money in this terrible Depression year.

Navin was strapped for cash himself, and $100,000 was a fortune. But something had to be done. He'd actually had another big name in mind for his new manager, the biggest of all, in fact. Babe Ruth. The Babe wanted a cut of the gate, though, and Navin wouldn't go for that.

Then Mack was on the phone.

Navin turned to Walter O. Briggs, an auto-parts-manufacturing millionaire who had bought a piece of the club, to get the funds. One week after this bombshell, Navin traded for veteran Washington outfielder Goose Goslin, another Depression distress sale. And the package was complete for 1934.

With Cochrane at the helm, Detroit broke away from the pack fast, fought off the Yankees, and cruised to the pennant with a 101–53 record, best in team history. Goslin joined Hank Greenberg and Charlie Gehringer as the G-Men. The entire heavy-hitting infield was nicknamed the Battalion of Death. Schoolboy Rowe, in his second year in the majors, reeled off 16 wins in a row on his way to 24, and Alvin "General" Crowder, who joined the team from Washington, chipped in five more down the stretch. Cochrane was not only Manager of the Year but also the league's MVP.

For the first time in 25 years, and the first time since Navin Field had opened, the World Series was back in Detroit. But the Tigers were up against a team that was every bit as ferocious as their own manager. The Cardinals' Gashouse Gang played the game for keeps, spikes and emotions high.

The Tigers were up 3–2 with the last two games to be played in Detroit. But the Dean brothers, Dizzy and Paul, were too much to handle, winning the final two games and all four of St. Louis' Series victories.

The seventh game turned into a fiasco, an 11–0 drubbing that featured one of the most infamous episodes in World Series history. After Joe Medwick spiked Tigers third baseman Marv Owen, fans in left field rioted, showering the St. Louis player with fruit and vegetables. With the contest already well in hand, Commissioner Kenesaw Landis halted play and ordered Medwick out of the game.

It was a brutal disappointment for the Tigers, as well as a black mark for the city. But in 1935, despite a

## TRIVIA

The 1934 World Series was the last one in which player-managers faced each other. Cochrane was one. Who was the other?

Answers to the trivia questions are on page 148.

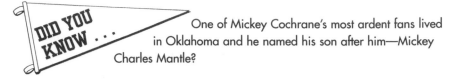

start that had them stuck in sixth place in late May, the Tigers came back to the Series for one more try.

All the G-Men drove in more than 100 runs (it was 170 for Greenberg), and Tommy Bridges, who had a curveball for every occasion, won 21. Every major league team had won a championship by now except for four—the Browns, Phillies, Dodgers, and Detroit. Surely, it would be the Tigers' turn at last.

But in Game 2 against the Cubs, the angry fate that seemed to ambush the Tigers in every Series struck again. After Greenberg's first-inning homer keyed an 8–3 win, evening up the Series at a game apiece, the Detroit slugger broke his hand in a collision at home plate. Owen had to shift to first base, and a seldom-used sub, Flea Clifton, was rushed in to play third. It looked like another prelude to disaster.

The Tigers won the next two, however, to go up 3–1. The Cubs took the fifth game, and with Bridges on the mound at home in Game 6 the score was tied 3–3 in the ninth. Chicago's Stan Hack led off with a triple, but Bridges left him stranded on third. Then the long wait finally ended.

Cochrane started the bottom of the ninth with a single. Gehringer sent a shot down the first-base line, but Phil Cavarretta knocked it down to make a play at the bag. Then it was Goslin's turn. The veteran looped a dying-quail single to right and Cochrane, appropriately enough, raced around third to score the winning run. Detroit exploded in joy. The World Series was theirs. The Depression-battered city celebrated deep into the night, horns honking and impromptu dances snaking throughout the downtown area. No one could ever remember anything like it.

But nothing that golden can stay. Greenberg sat out most of the 1936 season with his injured hand. Cochrane requested a trade for his old Philadelphia buddy, Al Simmons, but he was a poor fit for the Tigers. They fell further and further behind the Yankees and in mid-June Cochrane collapsed, landing in the hospital with what was described as a nervous breakdown. He stayed away from the team for a month, but soon after his return he suffered a relapse and was done for the season.

In 1937 he tried again and for a while it seemed the old magic was working. Greenberg was healthy and the Tigers started winning once more. But at Yankee Stadium in May, Cochrane lost a pitch from New York's Bump Hadley in the glare of white shirts. It fractured his skull in three places. He never played again.

He returned in 1938 as a bench manager. But the flame had died. He had to be actively involved in the game to be effective. He made mistakes, errors in judgment he never would have committed when he was on the field. By August the team was below .500 and he was fired.

There will never be a leader quite like Cochrane again in Detroit. For the Tigers fans of this era, Mickey was all that a manager should be, and every Detroit team that came afterward was only a pale imitation of the real thing.

After all, they put a plaque on the stadium wall honoring Cobb. But they named the street that ran behind home plate for Cochrane.

# Over the Roof

One million. It's a paltry number as baseball attendance goes these days. A team that only draws one million fans in a season can barely hope to survive—much less compete. Not when 2 million is regarded as pretty good and 3 million is the gold standard.

But when the Tigers drew 1.03 million in 1935, it was the most in the history of Navin Field. It got Walter O. Briggs to thinking. If Detroit can do this in a ballpark that seated 40,000, what would it do in a stadium of 55,000?

He had the chance to find out sooner than he knew.

Little more than a month after winning the club's first World Series, Frank Navin went out for a ride on one of his favorite horses. He never came back. The man who had owned the Tigers for 25 years fell from the saddle dead of a heart attack. His mausoleum in a Detroit cemetery is still guarded by carved stone tigers.

Navin's death and the Series triumph seemed to punctuate an era in Tigers history. Briggs, his partner, bought out Navin's shares and became sole owner. Within two years, he had transformed the aging ballpark into Briggs Stadium.

Navin Field was open behind right field and single-decked in left. Briggs added an upper deck all the way around the stadium, making it entirely enclosed. The effect was magical. Coming in from the streets of the city, you ascended a series of ramps to the second deck. Only then could you see the field, spread out before you like a pristine meadow. No one who saw it as a child will ever forget the sight.

The park was a hitter's delight. Ted Williams called it the best background in baseball, and a 1950s poll of sluggers by *Baseball Digest* validated his opinion. Center field was a forbidding 440 feet from home plate. But it was just 325 feet down the right-field line, and the overhanging second deck even shortened that length a little. But it was the power alleys that pleased the hitters—only 370 feet in right and 365 in left.

Above it all was the roof, 94 feet above the playing surface. Clearing it in right, and occasionally in left, became one of the most famous measures of a monster home run in the big leagues.

*Tiger Stadium at the peak of its glory, packed for Opening Day, 1961. The overhanging upper deck in right field presented one of the most tempting home-run targets in all of baseball.*

IF ONLY ... Baseball had integrated sooner, the Tigers might have signed Turkey Stearnes. He was a top slugger and brilliant center fielder for the Detroit Stars of the Negro Leagues and was voted into the Hall of Fame in 2000.

Before the second deck was built, the longest homer in the ballpark's history was hit by Babe Ruth. It supposedly left the park in right, traveled across Trumbull on the fly, and landed in the middle of the lumberyard on the other side of the street. Some observers said it carried over 600 feet, but that's just a guess.

Clearing the roof, however, left little doubt. It had to go 500 feet to gain a trajectory of that height over that distance.

Williams was the first to do it. It was in 1939, the rookie year for the Boston hitter, and it helped make his reputation as the game's emerging superstar. Many people believe he did it again two years later, with the walk-off homer that ended the 1941 All-Star Game. But that one crashed against the third deck and didn't leave the park.

Same with Reggie Jackson's gasp-inducing blast in the 1971 All-Star Game. It hit the base of the light tower on the roof in right center and came back onto the field. A foot or two to either side and it would have cleared everything, and maybe even matched Ruth's legendary blow.

Actually, it took 17 years before another hitter emulated Williams's feat, and it was the man who made "tape-measure homer" part of the baseball lingo. Mickey Mantle did it in 1956—and then cleared it twice more in the next four years.

The all-time champ at this power display, however, was Norm Cash. He became the third man to clear the roof during his breakout season of 1961—and then did it three more times the following year. Two of them came within three days of each other. That was a single-season record.

Jason Thompson, however, did it twice within a month in 1977, leading Tigers' broadcaster Ernie Harwell to nickname him "Rooftop."

Kirk Gibson cleared it three times in his career, and by the time the ballpark closed, even lesser lights, such as Chad Kreuter and Melvin Nieves, had placed roof jobs on their resumes. A total of 29 shots left the stadium by that route in the 62 seasons it stood as a target.

Clearing the left-field roof, which was even farther from the plate, was a tougher act to pull off. It only happened four times. Harmon Killebrew was the first in 1962. Frank Howard, Cecil Fielder, and Mark McGwire—long ball paragons all—did it, too.

The other great landmark of the ballpark was the flagpole, planted right in front of the "440" sign in dead center. Balls that caromed off the pole above the height of the adjacent fence were home runs. No tally was kept of that, but old timers can remember Boston's Dom DiMaggio balancing himself on the flagpole's base to bring down a home-run bound drive by Rudy York in the 1940s.

Briggs's seating expansion worked out well. He set another attendance record in the pennant-winning year of 1940. Even during wartime, when almost all able-bodied men held down day jobs during the afternoon, he managed to draw 923,000 fans in 1944.

Since 1945, the Tigers have dropped below one million in attendance just three times, and not at all since 1964. It is the third longest such streak in the big leagues, behind the Los Angeles Dodgers and the St. Louis Cardinals. Even the lordly Yankees cannot match it.

By the time the park closed, however, alterations had shrunk seating capacity to around 43,000. The philosophy had changed. It now is believed that a scarcity of seats induces fans to buy tickets in advance and boosts attendance.

While Briggs knew how to make his ballclub pay off, he was not regarded as one of the more progressive owners in the game. The Tigers were the last team besides the Cubs to play night baseball at home. They didn't turn on the lights until 1948, and for many years limited such games to less than a dozen a year.

More harmful, Briggs discouraged team officials from signing African Americans. The policy was a disaster for the Tigers. While

By the
NUMBERS

58,369—Largest baseball crowd ever in Detroit, for a doubleheader with the Yankees in 1947.

# TRIVIA

**Only three pitchers gave up two over-the-roof home runs.
Who were they?**

*Answers to the trivia questions are on page 148.*

Cleveland and Chicago rose in the standings with talented black athletes, the Tigers stagnated. Not until ownership passed from the Briggs family, in 1957, did a black player take the field with the Tigers. But Detroit's minority fans were not fooled. Ozzie Virgil, they pointed out, was from the Dominican Republic. It wasn't the same thing. Only when Jake Wood and Billy Bruton became starters in 1961 did things really change. But an aura of distrust of the team's intentions lingered for many years in the black community. It did not dissipate until the enormously popular Gates Brown and Willie Horton arrived in the mid-1960s and the team was fully embraced by African Americans.

# Bobo the Great

You could call him a journeyman, but that wouldn't begin to do justice to Bobo Newsom's baseball itinerary.

He was the game's Marco Polo. He played for 17 different teams in the majors and minors, including five separate stays with Washington. Senators owner Clark Griffith refused to be in the same room alone with Newsom because he was afraid "he'll talk me into trading for him again."

Newsom began his wanderings in Brooklyn in 1929 and they didn't end until he was 46 years old with the Philadelphia Athletics in 1953. And for one brief shining season he was probably the best pitcher in baseball. He came within a hair of pitching the Tigers to the 1940 world championship, and in so doing became a tragic hero.

"Everybody was 'Bobo' to him," recalled Hal Newhouser, "whether you were Hank Greenberg or a punk kid like me. He just couldn't keep anybody's name straight. So we just called him Bobo right back."

"He was overpowering in that one season," said Greenberg. "He threw what they later would call a slider, and no one could catch up to it. He even got Joe DiMaggio out with it a few times, although Joe hit him as well as anyone in the league. Better than I did when I had to face him. He'd keep it low and on the outside corner and I couldn't do a thing with it."

He even gave Ted Williams trouble.

"That fastball would come out of a whirlwind of arms and legs and you just couldn't pick it up until it was right at the plate," Williams said.

*Hank Greenberg is greeted by his teammates after slamming a home run in
an 8–0 rout of Cincinnati in Game 5 of the 1940 World Series. Bobo Newsom's
shutout brought the Tigers within one game of the championship...but it
wasn't to be.*

Newsom always had been classified as a horse, a decent pitcher
who would rack up lots of innings for his team. He'd even won 20
games for the lowly Browns in 1938, although he accomplished it
with an earned-run average of over 5.00—which made it difficult.

He led the league in losses four times and in walks twice. He was
regarded as a clown, a braggart, one of the game's true characters.

Once, he was pitching for Washington and a line drive caught
him on the leg.

"I think it's broken," he told manager Bucky Harris when he got back to the dugout. Harris immediately jumped up and waved to the bullpen to get someone ready.

"What are you doing?" said a genuinely puzzled Newsom. "I said it was broken. I didn't say I was dead."

Then he went back out and finished the ballgame.

But when he came to the Tigers, near the start of the 1939 season, Bobo suddenly hit his stride, finishing with a 20–11 overall record. Detroit was rebuilding from the 1935 championship team. Greenberg and Charlie Gehringer remained and so did Tommy Bridges, Pete Fox, and Schoolboy Rowe. But they had traded pitcher Elden Auker and two others for veteran Pinky Higgins at third and shortstop Billy Rogell for Dick Bartell at short. Young stars like Barney McCosky and catcher Birdie Tebbetts were producing. With Rudy York at first they had a second big slugger to go along with Greenberg. Newhouser was also on the pitching staff but was not yet the dominating Hall of Famer of a few years later. He was still a rookie, struggling with his control, and he never even got into a Series game in 1940.

The Tigers snapped the Yankees streak of four straight championships and edged out Cleveland for the pennant in the last weekend of the season. It had been a nasty race, with Tigers players hanging baby clothes from their dugout to taunt the "crybaby" Indians. Cleveland had complained about the disciplinary actions of its manager, ex-Tiger Ossie Vitt.

Rather than matching Newsom against Bob Feller in the final decisive series, manager Del Baker started a rookie, Floyd Giebell, instead. It was just his second big-league start, but he outdueled Cleveland's 27-game winner to clinch the pennant. Giebell never won another game in the majors.

**DID YOU KNOW . . .** The Tigers have held spring training in Lakeland, Florida, ever since 1934, with the exception of three years during World War II when travel restrictions made it impossible? It is the longest relationship in baseball between a team and a spring-training site.

**By the NUMBERS**

**.000**—Flea Clifton's batting average as a starter in four World Series games after being pressed into service in 1935 as an emergency replacement for Hank Greenberg.

But Newsom was the real difference. He went 21–5, even though he missed nearly the entire month of July with an injury. After all the years of clowning, he was now a very serious star.

It seemed as if the entire town of Hartsville, South Carolina, came up to Cincinnati to watch their old pal Bobo pitch in the Series. His dad, Henry, was in the stands for the opener as Newsom beat the Reds, 7–2. It was only the second time he'd seen his son pitch a big-league game. Then it was time to party.

The celebration lasted well into the night. When it was over, Henry Newsom returned to his hotel room after the happiest day of his life and died of a heart attack. When the Tigers went back to Detroit for the rest of the Series, Bobo went home to bury his father. Baker told him to take all the time he needed. He was scheduled to start Game 5, but everyone would understand if he wasn't there.

Instead, Bobo returned to Briggs Stadium and pitched an emotional three-hit shutout "for my dad."

The Reds evened the series in Game 6, and with just one day's rest Newsom was sent out to win the deciding game. He nearly did it, too. Clinging to a 1–0 lead in the seventh, however, he gave up back-to-back doubles to Frank McCormick and Jimmy Ripple.

McCormick had held up, thinking Ripple's ball might be caught, and Dick Bartell had a play on him at the plate on the relay. But he didn't see it until it was too late and the game was tied. A sacrifice fly brought in Ripple with the go-ahead run. The Tigers could not break through against Paul Derringer, and the Reds had an upset championship.

Bobo could never recapture the magic. After showing up at spring training in 1941 with a new convertible that played "Hold That Tiger" on its horn, he lost 20 games. The next

**TRIVIA**

A Cleveland Indians Hall of Famer made his only trip to the World Series as a member of the 1940 Tigers. Who was he?

*Answers to the trivia questions are on page 148.*

year he was again dealt to Washington and resumed his journeying. He never won more than 14 games in a season afterward.

At the end, he lost 11 more games than the 211 he won, and Bobo has slowly faded from baseball's memory. But it had been a great ride.

"They told me that if I'd kept my mouth shut I could have been a better pitcher," he said after his retirement. "But there were Bobos out there who won twice as many games as me and made less money. So who was the clown?"

# Prince Hal

Hal Newhouser was a riddle inside a puzzle. The young left-hander had all the stuff in the world, everything it took to win in the majors, yet it seemed he was going backward.

Many years later, Ted Williams sat on the honorees' platform at Cooperstown and tried to display with his hands how Newhouser's curveball had plunged viciously as it reached the hitting zone. The occasion was Prince Hal's induction into the Hall of Fame in 1992.

It had taken a long time for him to get there. Far too long in the minds of many. But the trip may not have been made at all if it hadn't been for an obscure minor league catcher who later became a great big-league manager. Paul Richards turned Newhouser into a dominating pitcher.

Newhouser was a Detroit native, a big fan favorite out of the local sandlots. He had reached the majors at the age of 19 and his potential seemed limitless. He was 9–9 in that first year and it appeared he would be a star before he had his first legal drink.

But a peculiar thing happened. His record got worse every year: 9–11; 8–14; 8–17. He walked more hitters than he struck out most seasons. He was hard to hit, but all those walks had runners on base against him constantly and the losses kept mounting.

When starting catcher Birdie Tebbetts left for military duty after 1942, the Tigers acquired Richards out of desperation. The 35-year-old Texan had bounced around the minors for eight years after three brief stints in the bigs, where he never hit as much as .200. But he was supposed to handle pitchers well, and there was a war on. Every available body was needed in the majors.

The top two marks for consecutive games played with the Tigers belong to Charlie Gehringer? It was 511 straight between 1927 and 1931, and then 504 from 1932 to 1935. Next in line is Rocky Colavito with 458.

Newhouser was draft-exempt because of a heart valve problem. Newly named manager Steve O'Neill, a terrific catcher himself in his playing days, believed that maybe all Newhouser needed was an old hand to steady him.

Richards soon learned that Newhouser's biggest problem was in his head. He could not pitch over mistakes, glaring at teammates when they made an error behind him. He was at war with the press, snapping at the most innocuous questions. The other Tigers detested him.

Richards waged a campaign to get him calmed down and thinking positive. Then it all clicked. In 1944 he was a changed pitcher, a different man. He and Dizzy Trout combined to win 56 games, and the Tigers lost the pennant by a single game.

The next year was even better. He went 25–9, won the league's ERA title with a 1.81 mark, and for the second straight season was named Most Valuable Player. He is still the only pitcher to win the award in consecutive seasons.

But some were convinced his record was tainted. The war had taken away so much. Williams was gone, and so were Hank Greenberg, Joe DiMaggio, Bob Feller—great talents at the peak of their careers. There is no telling what their final records would have looked like if they had not lost those years.

The accusation went that Newhouser was pitching against pale replacements. Even the pitiful St. Louis Browns had won the pennant in 1944 and what does that tell you? So why should this man's achievements be recognized as worthy of Cooperstown?

Over the years, Newhouser heard it all, and he bristled.

"All the stars came back in 1946, and I went 26–9," he argued. "I led the league in ERA again and struck out 275 guys. How can they say I was just a wartime player? I was a pitcher whose career happened to peak during the war years.

*Hal Newhouser's big windup and nasty curveball baffled hitters throughout the 1940s. He is pictured here in his rookie year of 1939, fresh off the sandlots of Detroit.*

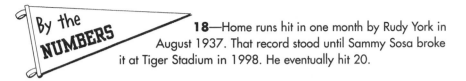

**18**—Home runs hit in one month by Rudy York in August 1937. That record stood until Sammy Sosa broke it at Tiger Stadium in 1998. He eventually hit 20.

"I really felt that I shortened my career because I was trying to do too much in those years right after the war. I wanted to show them all. But look at the record."

Newhouser remained among the league's top pitchers for another five years. He and Feller, his great rival with the Indians, were matched in several duels and filled ballparks on both sides of Lake Erie. But by 1951 his arm was dead and his career on the downslide. He had not yet reached his 30th birthday.

In 1945, however, he was at the pinnacle. Greenberg came back from the war in midseason and was his old self, driving in 60 runs in 78 games. Rudy York was still at first base, just like in the good years. Even ageless Tommy Bridges came back from the service in time to pitch in his fourth Series with Detroit.

Other than that, though, the '45 Tigers were a hodgepodge of aging veterans and glorified minor leaguers. Second baseman Eddie Mayo represented one aspect. The 35-year-old was a long-term minor leaguer who had shown little in previous shots. But this season he led the team in hitting at .285 and was its sparkplug.

Then there was Chuck Hostetler. Playing in the World Series at the age of 42, he fell down rounding third with the potential winning run in Game 6 and was thrown out. The Cubs won in 12 innings and forced a seventh game. It was that sort of thing that clinched the reputation of this Series as the worst ever played. It probably wasn't all that awful, but the war had been over for two months and fans were impatient for the real stars to return.

Hostetler's flop meant that Newhouser had to come out for the seventh game at Wrigley Field. He already had split two decisions and hadn't pitched all that well. He would have just two days of rest.

But the Cubs sent out Hank Borowy, who had pitched four innings of relief in Game 6. He never got a single hitter out this time.

Richards came to bat with the bases loaded in the first inning against reliever Paul Derringer, the pitcher who had beaten the Tigers in the deciding Series game in 1940. This time, Richards

All-1940s Tigers Team

| Position | Name |
| --- | --- |
| First Baseman | Rudy York |
| Second Baseman | Eddie Mayo |
| Shortstop | Eddie Lake |
| Third Baseman | George Kell |
| Outfielder | Hank Greenberg |
| Outfielder | Hoot Evers |
| Outfielder | Barney McCosky |
| Catcher | Birdie Tebbetts |
| Pitcher | Hal Newhouser |
| Pitcher | Dizzy Trout |

tagged him for a bases-clearing double. The aging catcher who had been obtained primarily to counsel Newhouser handed his protégé a 5–0 lead.

Again Newhouser was a bit shaky, giving up 10 hits. But he went the distance, and the Tigers won it coasting, 9–3. They were champions again.

Newhouser's arm problems resulted in his being dealt to Cleveland to join his old adversary, Feller. In 1954 they were both aging warriors on a team that was swept by the Giants in the Series. Newhouser faced two hitters in Game 4 and couldn't retire either one, and Feller never got into a game at all.

Newhouser was cut from the team early the following season and retired, going into a banking career in Detroit. Then he waited for the call that wouldn't come from Cooperstown. Feller was voted in almost immediately after his retirement in 1962. But it took 30 more years before Newhouser joined him there.

The wartime stigma took that long to shake.

# Midcentury Blues

The Tigers knew that the 1945 pennant was a bit of a fluke. A quick overhaul of the team was needed. Fortunately, some old familiar faces were coming back from the service and the farm system was producing new ones.

No two returnees were greeted with higher expectations than Barney McCosky and Dick Wakefield. The two outfielders were emerging stars before leaving for the service. They were to be the foundation of the revamped Tigers.

Funny how things turn out. The future got to Detroit by a less predictable route.

Slugger Rudy York was traded to Boston to make way for the new order, and Hank Greenberg was traded shortly thereafter. Despite leading the league with 44 homers and 127 RBIs, his batting average tailed off in 1946. The Tigers refused to pay the 35-year-old star the $80,000 he demanded, dealing him to Pittsburgh instead.

But it quickly became apparent that the two anticipated returnees were not the same players they used to be. McCosky, a solid .300 hitter in four prior seasons, couldn't get above .200. Worse yet, he seemed to have lost his speed and extra-base power.

Wakefield was an even more severe disappointment. The first bonus baby in history, the University of Michigan star had been signed for a mind-boggling $55,000. It looked like a great investment when he racked up 200 hits as a rookie in 1943. He left the team for the military the next year hitting .355 with a strong home-run stroke.

Wakefield supposedly ran into Ted Williams when both were in uniform and offered to bet him on which one would have the higher batting average when they returned. Williams declined the

**By the NUMBERS**

**12**—Home runs hit by the Tigers and White Sox to set a single-game record. In fact, the same two teams did it twice: once on May 28, 1995, at Tiger Stadium, and again on July 2, 2002, at Comiskey Park. Detroit's last two homers in the 2002 game came with two outs in the ninth inning.

bet. Good thing for Wakefield. Williams would have won by 74 points in 1946.

Wakefield never came close to his former promise and was finally traded to the Yankees. But the Tigers made honey out of vinegar in the case of McCosky. He was traded to Philadelphia for a young infielder who had not hit very much in the majors but had a great glove.

It turned out to be among the best deals the Tigers ever made. George Kell found his batting eye as soon as he hit town. He never finished below .300 in six full seasons with the Tigers, spraying line drives to every section of the ballpark. Despite the fact that he was playing on two wobbly knees, his defensive skills at third base were as good as advertised. It was a career that led him to Cooperstown.

Kell won the batting title in 1949, edging out Williams by .0002 of a point, the closest such race in history. He actually went ahead on the final day with two hits. While the game was still in progress, the pressbox sent word to the Tigers dugout that Williams had gone hitless. But Kell insisted on taking his last turn at bat. When the batter ahead of him hit into a double play, however, the season ended and Kell had won.

He struck out all of 13 times that season, still the record for the fewest by the winner of a batting title.

The farm system also began sending forth its promised payload. An entire outfield showed up. Hoot Evers came first, and then Vic Wertz, who became a legitimate home-run threat. Johnny Groth turned in a great rookie year in 1949. Suddenly the Tigers attack was formidable once more. All three hit over .300 in 1950.

Hal Newhouser and Dizzy Trout were joined by veteran Fred Hutchinson and young Art Houtteman, another product of the Detroit sandlots, on the pitching staff. Trades brought in veteran infielders Jerry Priddy and Don Kolloway.

*In one of the neatest trades Detroit ever made, George Kell was swiped from the A's to become the finest third baseman in team history. He won the batting title in 1949 and was outstanding on defense.*

IF ONLY . . . Detroit never had made the trade with Chicago
for Aaron Robinson in 1949. It went down as the worst
in franchise history. Billy Pierce went on to win 211 games, while
Robinson lasted a bit more than two seasons with the Tigers.

The only part missing in the equation was a good catcher.
General manager Billy Evans thought he knew where to find one. He
sent one of his young pitchers to the White Sox in return for Aaron
Robinson. The cast was complete.

The Tigers had been winning pennants every five years—1935,
1940, 1945. It looked like the 1950 team had come together right on
schedule.

The Yankees came to town in late June for a big series. In a wild
game before a crazed full house, the Tigers rallied from behind.
Trout, always a decent hitter with 20 career home runs, hit a grand
slam. Then Evers won it in the ninth, 10–9, with a two-run, inside-
the-park homer. Eleven home runs were hit in the game by nine
different players on both sides—setting a record at the time.

When Houtteman stopped New York the next night, Detroit's
lead stretched to 3 games and it seemed they were on their way.

But the Yankees did what the Yankees always seemed to do.
They brought Whitey Ford up from the minors in midseason, he
went 9–1, and they caught the Tigers in September for the pennant.
In a decisive series with Cleveland, Robinson neglected to see that
there was no force-play at the plate and did not put the tag on the
runner sliding in with the winning run. Detroit never recovered from
what became known as "Robby's Rock."

Still it seemed that the Tigers were loaded, set to challenge the
Yankees for years to come. It never happened. Manager Red Rolfe,
aloof most of the time, lost control of the team. The pitchers turned
old in a hurry. A widely discussed article about the Tigers in *Look
Magazine* was headlined "Fat Cats Don't Win Pennant."

The Tigers went nowhere in 1951. Attendance plunged by
800,000 from the previous season's record of 1.9 million. The front
office was faced with high salaries for a pack of unproductive stars.
When the team finished fifth, 25 games off the lead, owner Walter O.
Briggs turned to an old hero to fix things. Charlie Gehringer came

back with the title of vice president and cleaned house. Within two years, every starter on the 1951 team, with the exception of pitcher Ted Gray, was gone.

Detroit fans were shocked. This was a bloodbath. Never in the history of the franchise had they seen anything like this. In just one blockbuster

Answers to the trivia questions are on page 148.

**TRIVIA**

A month after coming to the Tigers in a 1952 trade, he set a record by getting 12 straight hits. Who is he?

deal, Gehringer sent off Kell, Evers, Trout, and shortstop Johnny Lipon. Four stars gone in one fell swoop. Newspapers were flooded with phone calls from angry, disbelieving fans.

But Gehringer was doing more than shuffling bodies around. He was also preparing the groundwork for a front-office reorganization that would restore stability to the franchise. Among those he brought in was Jim Campbell, who would direct the Tigers to two world championships in his 31-year run as general manager and vice president.

Briggs passed from the scene, too, passing away in 1952 and leaving the franchise in the hands of his son, Spike. Over the previous 43 years, the Tigers had been owned by just two men, Frank Navin and Briggs. Both were serious businessmen, while Spike had earned the reputation as a bit of a playboy.

The times were changing in a hurry for the Tigers.

# The Long and Short of It

His official entry in *The Baseball Encyclopedia* says that Eddie Gaedel threw left-handed. It's hard to know where they got that information. Because in the only ballgame Gaedel played, either in the minors or in the majors, he walked, and then was immediately removed for a pinch runner. He probably never even put on a mitt.

Gaedel was the central figure in one of baseball's most bizarre moments. He was the 3'7" little person who came to bat for the St. Louis Browns in a game against the Tigers in 1951. The photograph of him in the batter's box, with catcher Bob Swift on his knees trying to present a target to the pitcher, is among the most widely reproduced in the game's history. For those Detroit fans who believe that everything happens to the Tigers, Gaedel clinched the case.

As a publicity gimmick by Browns president Bill Veeck, it was a master stroke. He signed the 26-year-old Gaedel to a valid contract and filed it routinely with the league office late on a Friday, knowing it would not be scrutinized until Monday.

Gaedel popped out of a cake between games of a Sunday doubleheader in a Browns uniform with the number 1/8 on the back. Then Veeck sent him in as a pinch-hitter to start the bottom of the first. When the plate umpire challenged the move, manager Zach Taylor produced the contract.

In his autobiography, *Veeck as in Wreck*, Veeck wrote that Gaedel told him he might swing if he got a good pitch. "I told him if he did that I had stationed a sniper in the stands," said Veeck.

Swift advised pitcher Bob Cain to "keep it low," although it is hard to see what alternative he had. Cain was laughing so hard he never came close to throwing a strike to Gaedel's one-and-a-half-inch strike zone. He walked on four pitches, and the next day his contract was voided by humorless league officials.

It was certainly the strangest incident in a most peculiar period in Detroit's history. The next season they finished dead last for the first time ever.

Even then, however, there was something worth remembering. During the course of a season in which Virgil Trucks won only five games, two of them were no-hitters. Trucks had been a star on the staff since 1942. Eligibility rules had been waived for him when he came out of the military late in 1945 so he could pitch in the World Series. He responded by going nine innings and beating the Cubs, 4–1, in Game 2. An injury that took him out of the rotation in 1950 was one of the main reasons the Tigers lost out to the Yankees that year.

In the generally awful 1951 season, he had gone 13–8. But along with the rest of the team his record went into the ash can in 1952. He would finish 5–19. Only the fact that his teammate Art Houtteman lost 20 kept him from leading the league in that odious department. The team was so last it finished 14 games behind the seventh-place Browns.

But on May 15, Trucks took the mound at Tiger Stadium to face Washington. This was a pretty good Senators team, with a pair of two-time batting champs, Mickey Vernon and Pete Runnels, in the lineup, along with Jackie Jensen.

Through the top of the ninth, Trucks had not given up a hit. Trouble was Washington's Bob Porterfield was pitching a three-hit shutout. Then with two outs in the bottom of the ninth, Tiger Vic Wertz put one against the facing of the upper deck in right and Trucks won his no-hitter. Trucks was so excited he jumped to his feet and almost knocked himself out on the dugout ceiling.

A bit more than three months later, Trucks did it again. This time the setting was the center stage, Yankee Stadium, against a

**DID YOU KNOW . . .** The Tigers have been no-hit 12 times, losing 11 of them? In 1967, though, despite having a no-hitter thrown at them by Steve Barber and Stu Miller, they beat Baltimore, 2–1, on walks and errors.

team sweeping to its fourth straight world championship. It was a lineup with Mickey Mantle (who was hitting leadoff), Yogi Berra, and Hank Bauer—with Johnny Mize as a pinch-hitter.

Once more, Trucks encountered a pitcher almost as sharp as he was. Bill Miller had the Tigers blanked through six, but a double by Walt Dropo and a single by Steve Souchock got in the run. Even this game had a strange twist. Yankee Phil Rizzuto reached base early when Tigers shortstop Johnny Pesky seemed to bobble the ball as he was taking it out of his glove. The scorer ruled it an error, then changed his mind and called it a hit.

*Showman Bill Veeck outdid himself when he sent Eddie Gaedel to bat against the Tigers in a 1951 game with the Browns. The little man drew a walk and was taken out for a pinch runner. Humorless league officials voided his contract the next day.*

But as the innings and Trucks kept rolling along, the scorer started coming under pressure to reconsider. Finally, he made the unusual move of calling the Detroit dugout to ask Pesky. "You could have made that play," Pesky told him. That did it. The decision was changed again, and when it was posted on the scoreboard even the New York fans cheered.

# TRIVIA

**Besides Virgil Trucks and his two no-hitters, how many other Detroit pitchers have thrown no-hit games?**

*Answers to the trivia questions are on page 148.*

Oddly enough, Houtteman came within a few outs of pitching a third no-hitter for the Tigers that year. Suitcase Simpson singled in the ninth for Cleveland to break up that one.

This was not the first time a pitcher had double no-hitters in a season. Allie Reynolds did it for the Yankees just the previous year, and Johnny Vander Meer got his back-to-back jobs in 1938 for the Reds. Nolan Ryan also accomplished it for the Angels in 1973. But all those pitchers were having good years. The no-nos didn't account for 40 percent of their total wins.

As a reward, Trucks was traded to the equally horrible Browns during the off-season.

But the light at the end of the tunnel was already visible by the end of the dreadful last-place season. The Tigers signed shortstop Harvey Kuenn out of the University of Wisconsin, and in the last month of the year he hit .325. Next season he would be Rookie of the Year.

Then the Tigers traded for Ray Boone from Cleveland. He moved in at third base and combined with Kuenn to give Detroit one of the best-hitting infields in the game. The Tigers also obtained veteran pitcher Steve Gromek, who had grown up in the area, in the same trade. He would anchor the pitching staff with an 18-win season in 1954.

There was still a long way to go, but it seemed the Tigers were becoming the Tigers once more.

# The Kid from Baltimore

If you had been in the Tigers clubhouse when he arrived, you would have wondered what all the fuss was about.

This skinny 18-year-old kid didn't look like much. He was just a few days past his senior prom at a Baltimore high school, and to make it worse he was a bonus baby. That meant under the new rules the team was going to be stuck with him for two years before he could go to the minors for seasoning.

As it turned out, Al Kaline never needed to get seasoned anywhere else. In one year he would be a regular and in two years a batting champion. He would play more games and hit more home runs than any Detroit player in history, and his election to Cooperstown was a slam dunk.

For the next 20 seasons he would be the face of the Tigers and the soul of the franchise. On good teams and bad, he was the constant star.

He played right field with a skill and exuberance that had rarely been seen on any field. The team had to remove a few dozen seats from the right-field corner of Briggs Stadium to protect their young star from injury. His range extended that much farther than any other man who had played out there for Detroit.

For the rest of the stadium's existence, the area would be called Kaline's Corner. The tradition is carried on even at Comerica Park. A sign indicates a portion of the right-field corner is still named for Kaline, even though it is in the upper deck.

"He stood out like a cat's eye in a dark room," said Ed Katalinas, who scouted and signed him for the Tigers. In the days before the common draft, the "bonus baby" rule was baseball's way of keeping the wealthier clubs from signing all the top prospects. The reasoning was that teams in a pennant race would not want to give up a roster spot to someone who probably would not play. In reality, many promising young players sat on a big-league bench for two wasted years and never regained their traction.

*The sweetest swing in the American League for many years belonged to Al Kaline. He arrived right out of high school and stayed for 22 seasons for a Hall of Fame career that turned him into a Detroit sports icon.*

**TOP 10**

### Career Batting Average

| | Player | BA |
|---|---|---|
| 1. | Ty Cobb | .368 |
| 2. | Harry Heilmann | .342 |
| 3. | Bob Fothergill | .337 |
| 4. | George Kell | .325 |
| 5. | Heinie Manush | .321 |
| 6. | Charlie Gehringer | .320 |
| 7. | Hank Greenberg | .319 |
| 8. | Gee Walker | .317 |
| 9. | Harvey Kuenn | .314 |
| 10. | Barney McCosky | .312 |

But the Tigers, coming off a horrendous last-place finish, did not figure to be in any kind of pennant race for the next few years. There was nothing to lose with Kaline.

Manager Fred Hutchinson was noted for his violent temper as a player. It was said that you could tell when he was knocked out of a game by the broken lightbulbs in the tunnel between the Tigers dugout and the clubhouse. As a manager, however, he had remarkable patience with young players, and he brought Kaline along at a comfortable pace.

In 1954 Hutch put him in the lineup and Kaline had a steady, if rather unspectacular, season—although, for a teenager, a .276 average in the majors may be considered somewhat spectacular.

By the next year Kaline was a superstar. He announced his arrival in an April game with Kansas City when he hit two home runs in one inning. He went on to get 200 hits for the only time in his career, drive in 102 runs, and hit .340. He was the youngest man ever to be batting champion, beating out Brooklyn's Pete Reiser by about three months.

"I never considered myself a power hitter," he said. "But when a pitcher made a mistake I made sure I was ready."

As a matter of fact, Kaline never hit more than 29 home runs in a season. But there were a lot of seasons. In what was shaping up as his best power year ever, in 1962, he fractured his collarbone while making a diving catch to save a ballgame at Yankee Stadium. He missed almost two months and still hit 29 homers. He would easily have made it to 40 that year, and thus removed a small irritant from his final résumé.

"I finished with over 3,000 hits [seven more, to be exact] and 399 home runs," he said. "When Carl Yastrzemski retired they announced that he was the first American Leaguer ever to get 3,000 hits and 400 homers. I never paid much attention to statistics, but that would have been nice.

"The Yankees were so good during most of my career that we didn't get into contention too often. I remember one game in New York, though, where I drove in all three of our runs and then took a home run away from Mickey [Mantle] by toppling into the right-field seats. The Yankees radio coverage went off the air saying they had won and one of the newspaper headlines the next day read 'Kaline 3, Yankees 2.'"

Kaline was less fond of a headline that appeared in *Sports Illustrated*, where he was featured on the cover photo with Harvey Kuenn. "It said 'He has the racket solved,'" said Kaline. "I never thought that way. I never considered myself in the same bracket as Mantle or Willie Mays, guys who were blessed with incredible skills. I had to work for it."

His stats, in fact, were never eye-popping, but few players were more respected by their peers. There was no one who American League pitchers wanted less to come to bat in a clutch situation late in the game.

"I never realized how great he was until I saw him play every day," said Johnny Podres after coming over from the Dodgers. "He just does everything great."

In his later years, Kaline was given the supreme accolade. Other players simply referred to him by his uniform number, 6.

By then, however, injuries limited his playing time and restricted his abilities as a hitter. His yearly batting

# TRIVIA

**Who did Al Kaline replace as Detroit's starting right fielder, and who replaced Kaline?**

*Answers to the trivia questions are on page 148.*

averages dipped and he finished his career just below .300. It is one of the few offensive categories in which he is not among the team's career top 10, usually trailing only Ty Cobb.

When the Tigers finally broke through to a pennant in 1968, a season in which injuries kept Kaline on the bench for two months, it was unthinkable that he would not be in the starting lineup for the World Series.

Manager Mayo Smith toyed with the idea of starting him at third, before deciding on the incredible gamble of playing center fielder Mickey Stanley at shortstop. All Al did was hit .379, lead the team in RBIs, and drive in the runs that brought the Tigers from behind in the fifth game and set the stage for their comeback victory in the Series.

When he called it a career in 1974, he simply ran off the field after his last at-bat at Tiger Stadium. No curtain call. No fuss. No drama.

Just a guy who had shown up to do his job every day since he was a kid, and happened to do it superlatively well.

# The Yankee Killer and Others

There really was no rational explanation for it. Sure, the jokers pointed out that Frank Lary hailed from Alabama and naturally had it in for anything with the word *Yankees* in it. But if it really was a rebel vendetta, he carried it a bit far.

In an era when the Yankees were the scourge of the American League, winning the pennant eight of the nine full seasons Lary spent with the Tigers, he treated them like a bunch of ham-and-eggers.

His career record against them was 27–13. Against the rest of the league over that same span it was 96–95.

Even Casey Stengel gave his grudging respect. The New York manager called him Bulldog. To the rest of the Tigers, though, he was Taters, a guy who would "borrow" the team bus in Florida one night because he needed to cross the county line to get a drink and had no other mode of transportation.

Mostly because of Lary, the Tigers always played the Yankees tough. Not that it did them much good. In the years they didn't finish in fifth place, they'd wind up in fourth.

The pinnacle came in 1958 when Lary beat them seven times. No one had beaten the Yankees seven times in a season since the dead-ball era. But the Tigers finished 15 games out of first place anyway.

Once he beat them by dropping down a squeeze bunt; another time he beat them on a home run in the ninth. It was simply uncanny.

It wasn't that he was a mediocrity. He was twice a 20-game winner, and in three All-Star appearances he never allowed an earned run. But the sight of the Yankees took him to another level entirely.

But eventually the piper had to be paid. In a bitterly cold early April game in 1962, he tripled against them and pulled a muscle as he ran out the hit. The injury didn't heal properly, he hurt his arm trying to come back too quickly, and he was never the same pitcher again.

Lary had many allies in his campaign against New York. Chief among them was Charlie Maxwell. He came from a little town named Lawton in western Michigan. But when radio announcer Van Patrick ascertained that it was located not too far from Paw Paw, Maxwell became "Old Paw Paw" on his broadcasts. It had a certain ring to it.

Maxwell had kicked around in the Boston farm system for several seasons and ended up in Detroit in 1956. Like so many left-handed hitters before and after him, he took one look at the stadium's right-field seats and fell in love. He would average 24 home runs and 82 RBIs the next five seasons and would become a huge fan favorite at Briggs Stadium.

But it was in 1959 that he had a Sabbath apotheosis. The Tigers got off to a 2–15 start that year and were wallowing in the swamps of ineptitude. Jimmie Dykes was brought in to manage the team. Maxwell was hitting .190 at the time. Dykes gave him a start in a doubleheader against the Yankees at Briggs Stadium, and he hit four consecutive home runs in the two games, as the Tigers swept.

The next week, he hit another big homer on Sunday. Patrick was ecstatic. "It's Old Paw Paw and his Sunday punch," he chirped into the microphone.

When Maxwell slammed a three-run Sunday shot at Yankee Stadium as the Tigers swept another doubleheader from New York, the day became part of his nickname.

Maxwell hit 31 home runs that year and 11 of them were on a Sunday. The Tigers, however, finished their standard fourth, 18 games off the pace (but only three behind New York in one of the only two years among the surrounding 10 that they failed to win the pennant).

These were frustrating seasons for Tigers fans. Their roster always seemed to be loaded. In 1956, for example, both Lary and Billy Hoeft were 20-game winners, while Maxwell, Al Kaline, Harvey Kuenn, and Ray Boone all hit over .300.

*Jim Bunning's slider made him one of the most feared pitchers in baseball in the 1950s and '60s. He pitched a no-hitter for the Tigers at Fenway Park and is one of the few pitchers to win 100 games in both the American and National Leagues.* Photo courtesy of Getty Images.

Computers were just coming into popular awareness then. A magazine fed some stats into one of the newfangled machines to predict the pennant winner for the next season. The computer said it would be the Tigers.

Detroit fans were ecstatic. Computers don't lie.

"You don't play the game with computers," said Yogi Berra, chillingly, when the magazine asked him for comment.

Darned if he wasn't right. The Tigers finished fourth, 20 games behind Yogi and his friends.

There was a scene in the movie *Peggy Sue Got Married* in which a bunch of the guys sit around at a party, going over the names on the Tigers pitching staff and figuring that they were a cinch to win the pennant. Any Detroit fan could have identified.

Jim Bunning was there, too. He went into the Hall of Fame wearing a Phillies cap, but he actually spent more seasons and won more games for the Tigers. He also prepared himself for his place in the U.S. Senate with some monumental contract battles with Detroit general manager Jim Campbell.

Then there was Kuenn, the best-hitting shortstop in the league. Only an average fielder with so-so speed, Kuenn hit everything on a

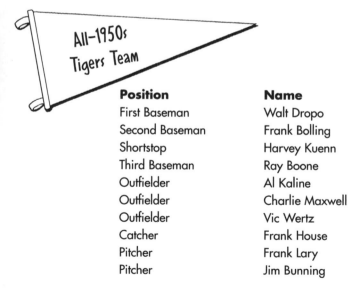

**All-1950s Tigers Team**

| Position | Name |
| --- | --- |
| First Baseman | Walt Dropo |
| Second Baseman | Frank Bolling |
| Shortstop | Harvey Kuenn |
| Third Baseman | Ray Boone |
| Outfielder | Al Kaline |
| Outfielder | Charlie Maxwell |
| Outfielder | Vic Wertz |
| Catcher | Frank House |
| Pitcher | Frank Lary |
| Pitcher | Jim Bunning |

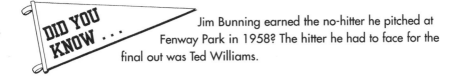

Jim Bunning earned the no-hitter he pitched at Fenway Park in 1958? The hitter he had to face for the final out was Ted Williams.

line. His strikeout totals were minuscule—just 13 in 656 at-bats in 1954. The Tigers eventually turned him into an outfielder and brought in Billy Martin to play shortstop.

That did wonders for Kuenn's batting average. In 1959 he hit .353 and became the Tigers 21st batting champ. But Martin didn't do much for the defense.

The Tigers of the late 1950s had no shortage of All-Star team selections, but somehow it never quite seemed to hang together. The sum was always less than the parts.

If only every day could have been a Sunday against the Yankees.

# The Rock and Stormin' Norman

It was a busy couple of years for Bill DeWitt as president of the Tigers. The team was sold by the Briggs family to a consortium of Michigan businessmen and they installed DeWitt, an experienced baseball man, to run it in 1959.

Among his first decisions was to change the name of the ballpark to Tiger Stadium. He would make other decisions that were far stranger. In mid-1960, for example, he traded managers even up. Jimmie Dykes went to Cleveland and Joe Gordon came to Detroit. Not that it made a difference. Neither club was going anywhere.

His biggest blockbuster, however, had come in spring training of that year. Days before the ballclub left Lakeland, he dealt Harvey Kuenn to the Indians for Rocky Colavito. Just a few days before that, DeWitt and Cleveland's general manager, Frank Lane, had pulled off another deal. This one attracted almost no attention at the time, but its implications reached even farther for the Tigers. DeWitt traded minor league infielder Steve Demeter for another utility player, first baseman Norm Cash. For Detroit, it was one of the steals of the century.

But the Kuenn-Colavito swap caused an immediate furor in both cities. It was a trade of a defending batting champion (Kuenn) for a defending home-run leader (Colavito). No one could recall anything like it.

"I traded a hamburger for a steak," chortled Lane. But Indians fans, who adored the handsome, power-hitting Colavito, were furious.

Despite Kuenn's seven years as a star in the Detroit lineup, Tigers fans enthusiastically embraced the deal. "Don't knock the Rock," became an overnight catchphrase at the ballpark.

**TOP 10**

### Tigers Home Runs in One Season

| | Player | HR | Year |
|---|---|---|---|
| 1. | Hank Greenberg | 58 | 1938 |
| 2. | Cecil Fielder | 51 | 1990 |
| 3. | Rocky Colavito | 45 | 1961 |
| 4. | Hank Greenberg | 44 t | 1946 |
| | Cecil Fielder | 44 t | 1991 |
| 6. | Hank Greenberg | 41 t | 1940 |
| | Norm Cash | 41 t | 1961 |
| 8. | Hank Greenberg | 40 t | 1937 |
| | Darrell Evans | 40 t | 1985 |
| 10. | Norm Cash | 39 | 1962 |

When Colavito lined a ball into the left-field seats on his first time up as a Tiger in newly renamed Tiger Stadium, their elation knew no bounds. But Detroit soon settled into its usual second division malaise—occasioning the trade of managers later that summer.

The Tigers had to wait one more year for the eruption. But when it came it was a doozie.

The team installed rookies Jake Wood and Steve Boros in the infield and swung a trade for veteran outfielder Billy Bruton and a dependable catcher in Dick Brown. The four new starters made an immediate impact.

Colavito followed up a fairly unimpressive first season in Detroit with a breakout year—45 homers and 140 RBIs.

But it was Cash who stunned the baseball world. Nothing in his past would have hinted at the sort of season he had. A multisport star at tiny Sul Ross State College, in west Texas, he had been signed by the White Sox and played sparingly during their pennant run in 1959. He played not at all for Cleveland, to whom he was dealt in the off-season, before being packed off to Detroit.

He actually led the Tigers in 1960 with a .286 average. But in '61, Cash broke the bank. He became Stormin' Norman, leading the

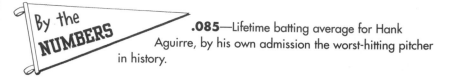

**.085**—Lifetime batting average for Hank Aguirre, by his own admission the worst-hitting pitcher in history.

league in hitting at .361, slamming 41 homers, and adding 132 RBIs. These were superstar numbers.

While the nation was transfixed on the historic home-run race between Roger Maris and Mickey Mantle of the Yankees, Cash and Colavito stayed almost even with the New York duo for most of the year.

They energized the rest of the team. Al Kaline was healthy and trailed only Cash in batting average. Frank Lary won 23, and Don Mossi, another player who had come over from Cleveland, gave the Tigers a dependable number three starter.

For most of the summer, the Tigers and Yanks were neck and neck. Then Detroit went into Yankee Stadium on Labor Day weekend and suffered the fate most contenders did on visits such as these.

On Friday night, Mossi was beaten, 1–0, on three dribblers through the infield with two outs in the ninth. The Tigers then lost the next two games, and the race was over.

Still, they finished with 101 wins, set an attendance record, and gave their fans a pennant race for the first time in 11 years and something to look forward to, as well. Then it went ker-flooey.

"The season I had was probably the worst thing that ever happened to me," Cash would lament in later years. "Everybody expected me to do it again, and no one can have that kind of season again—unless you're Ted Williams. I had some pretty good seasons in Detroit, but it was never enough."

He would become the prime target of the fans' wrath in Detroit, booed more than any other Tiger. Only Kaline, however, hit more career homers for the team than he did.

Colavito's run as a fan favorite was even shorter. He was always volatile, charging into the stands in Yankee Stadium in 1961 when he thought some fans were harassing members of his family. He was abrasive, as well.

His contract talks were thorny, as he demanded to be paid as much as Kaline. "What is he," asked the Rock, "a little tin god?" That did not go over well in Detroit. Nor did he ever approach the sort of season he'd had in 1961. Two years later Colavito was exiled to Kansas City.

Lary hurt his arm in 1962 and never came back from the injury. Manager Bob Scheffing, hailed as a genius during the pennant run, was sent up to the radio booth to keep Ernie Harwell company in 1963, and was replaced by veteran Chuck Dressen. Detroit fans reacted with disgust and stayed away from the park. In 1964 attendance fell all the way to 816,000, a low for the postwar years.

*Norm Cash can't connect with Bob Gibson's fastball in the opening game of the 1968 World Series. The first baseman was at the heart of the Tigers' lineup for more than a decade, one of the most popular players ever to wear the Detroit uniform.*

It seemed the turmoil was never ending, even tragic. In 1966 both Dressen and his successor as manager, Bob Swift, died—Dressen during the course of the season and Swift right after it.

The one positive factor was that a single owner had emerged from the consortium that purchased the team from the Briggs family and restored stability in the front office. John Fetzer, a broadcasting executive from Kalamazoo, bought out his partners in 1961.

Fetzer kept his hands off the baseball end of the operation, named Jim Campbell as his general manager, and told him to get busy restoring the Tigers farm system to the best in the game. Which he set about doing.

# Willie and Gates

He was a legend before he became a Tiger.

On the sandlots of Detroit they would look at where Willie Horton had hit the ball and shake their heads. No one in the history of the Northwestern Field diamonds had even come close to putting one on Grand River Avenue on the fly. Willie smashed a home run into the middle of the street.

In a high school all-star game, he crushed a ball into the upper deck of Tiger Stadium. There were pictures of him on the front of the sports page of both daily papers after that one. "Powerhouse Prep," read the headlines.

Everyone knew he was headed for the Tigers, and the fans could hardly wait. All Willie wanted to do was play ball for the team of his boyhood dreams. Well, maybe get in a little boxing, too.

"I loved to fight but my mom was dead set against it," he said. "So I'd go across the river to Canada and get in some amateur fights. But the TV station over there covered one of them and that station could be picked up in Detroit. My mom saw it, and that was the end of my boxing career.

"I beat some pretty good fighters, too. One of them even made the U.S. Olympic team in 1964."

Even when he played with the Tigers, Horton's strength and love of the fray were well known to his teammates.

"If a fight broke out," said Bill Freehan, "first you saw where Willie was and then you made sure you stayed out of his way."

*The Baseball Encyclopedia* lists him at 5'11", which is a good two inches too generous. During the prime of his career he weighed well over 200 pounds. But not much of it was fat. Willie was a rock.

Like most men who are confident of their own strength, he was also gentle. Some would say sensitive.

He was acutely aware of the fact that he was perceived as a representative of Detroit's black community, the first African American to become a star on the team. He neither sought nor wanted that role. It made him uncomfortable. But on the first day of the deadly 1967 riots he took it upon himself to go into the streets he knew so well and try to calm the situation. In the years of racial tension that followed, the pressures on him were sometimes unendurable. On one occasion he left the team and disappeared for a few days.

All he really wanted to do was hit baseballs hard, and that he did exceedingly well.

He had stepped right off the sidewalks of Detroit to become a hero, and that endeared him to everyone, white and black. Horton grew up in the same neighborhood as the artists who were making musical history at Motown Records, just a mile or two from the ballpark. The Supremes. The Temptations. The Four Tops. Martha and the Vandellas. They were all of a piece at this moment in time in the city, symbols of the way Detroit was changing.

He won the starting job in left field in 1965 with an outburst that became known as "Seven Games in May." An avalanche of extra-base hits and RBIs, including 10 RBIs in two games with four home runs at Boston, announced his arrival emphatically.

His father lived long enough to see his first big-league home run, coming off Hall of Famer Robin Roberts at the end of the 1963 season. He had been offered box seats by the Detroit dugout, but Clint Horton insisted on watching from his usual perch in the upper-deck center-field bleachers.

But when Willie's home run disappeared into the seats, he could restrain himself no longer. "That's my boy down there," he hollered. "That's my boy, Willie."

His companions were unimpressed. "If that's your boy down there," asked one of them, "what are you doing up here?"

By the mid-1960s, Willie's promise was fulfilled. He was the big right-handed cleanup hitter in the model of Hank Greenberg, Rudy York, and his own idol, Rocky Colavito.

The man he replaced as a starter in left was his best friend on the team. For the rest of his career, Gates Brown would be the team's pinch-hitter extraordinaire. His road to the big leagues had been rockier than Horton's, including a stretch of time in the Ohio State

*Raw power was Willie Horton's style. He was a local sandlot hero, and his massive home runs were the stuff of legend. He added to his lore as the slugging left-fielder for the Tigers through the '60s and '70s.*

**TOP 10**

## Tigers Pinch-Hits per Season

| | Player | Year | Pinch Hits |
|---|---|---|---|
| 1. | Bob Fothergill | 1929 | 19 |
| 2. | Gates Brown | 1968 | 18 |
| 3. | Sammy Hale | 1920 | 17† |
| | Vic Wertz | 1962 | 17† |
| 5. | Gates Brown | 1974 | 16 |
| 6. | Gus Zernial | 1958 | 15 |
| 7. | Billy Rhiel | 1932 | 13† |
| | Pat Mullin | 1953 | 13† |
| | Gates Brown | 1966 | 13† |
| | Dalton Jones | 1971 | 13† |

Penitentiary. No hometown acclaim and scouts knocking at the door for Gates. He got to town the hard way.

In time, though, his popularity was just as great as Willie's. When the Tiger Stadium crowd saw him start to stir in the dugout in the late innings and then come out to the on-deck circle to hit, the buzz grew to a roar before he ever reached the batter's box.

During the championship season of 1968, Gates was nearly miraculous. He pinch hit at a .462 pace and one Sunday in August, with the race narrowing, knocked in the winning run in both games of a doubleheader.

"It would have been nice if the designated hitter rule had come in when I was at my peak," he said. "But they always told me that my arm was too weak to play regularly in the outfield. I don't know how they'd know that since I never really got the chance to play, but that's what they said.

"When the DH finally came in, they used Al Kaline there. No one was gonna move Al Kaline aside in Detroit. But when he retired and it came to be my turn, it was already too late for me. I was done."

Gates was a little bigger than Willie but had the same stocky build. He hit with the same degree of power during his limited opportunities, and he was one of the fastest men on the team. And he could do no wrong at Tiger Stadium.

In one of the most touching moments of the 1968 season, in a city still bearing the open wounds of the riots, a Jewish business organization chose Gates as the man who best exemplified the spirit of the Tigers and presented him with a new car.

Healing can sometimes take strange forms. Both Willie and Gates played their parts.

# Going for 30

Midway through the madness, Ernie Harwell wrote a song about him. The refrain went: "You know there's not many like Denny McLain."

That qualified as the understatement of 1968.

McLain was a one-man carnival. Media and movie stars trailing in his wake. Crowds chanting his name at the ballpark. Headlines by the bushel.

The Tigers' race to their first pennant in 23 years almost got lost in the shadows as their young right-handed pitcher went after something that hadn't been done in 34 years.

Winning 30 games is the pitching equivalent of hitting .400. Since the demise of the dead ball, maybe it is even more difficult. Only three pitchers had accomplished it—Jim Bagby in 1920, Lefty Grove in 1931, Dizzy Dean in 1934.

A few had come close, including the Tigers' Hal Newhouser, who won 29 games in 1944. But this was another era, when television was creating instant national celebrities of sports figures.

And Denny soaked it all up like a sponge.

He played the organ in nightclubs. He flew his own plane, a hobby that won him the nickname of Sky King from the other Tigers. He said what was on his mind, and if it came out all wrong in the paper he didn't really care. He just went out every fourth day and blew people away.

He was a tough, square-jawed Irish kid from Chicago and he played the part. His persona had always been modified by the fact that he wore glasses. But when he showed up for spring training, the specs had been replaced by contacts. His hair was also bright orange—a result, he explained, of being out in the sun a lot.

At age 24, McLain was in his fourth season as a starter, but the road had a few turns in it. During Detroit's near miss of 1967, he had gone 17–16 and was ineffective in critical games. There were ugly rumors of involvement with the mob. A late-season injury, it was said, came as the result of a stomping by the boss of a local crime family. Denny said he had twisted the foot while jumping from his living room couch after awakening from a nap.

The Tigers were troubled and trolled for a trade during the off-season. But no deals were forthcoming and they brought him back for 1968. It may have been the greatest nontrade in franchise history.

*Denny McLain turned the world on its ear with his 31-win season in 1968, pitching the Tigers to the pennant. His performance off the field was just as newsworthy, and he was constantly in the headlines for his mouth as well as his arm.*

**TOP 10**

## Tigers Wins in One Season

| | Player | Year | Wins |
|---|---|---|---|
| 1. | Denny McLain | 1968 | 31 |
| 2. | George Mullin | 1909 | 29 t |
| | Hal Newhouser | 1944 | 29 t |
| 4. | Dizzy Trout | 1944 | 27 |
| 5. | Hal Newhouser | 1946 | 26 |
| 6. | Bill Donovan | 1907 | 25 t |
| | Ed Killian | 1907 | 25 t |
| | Hal Newhouser | 1945 | 25 t |
| | Mickey Lolich | 1971 | 25 t |

By early May he was 4–0, not all that spectacular but enough to get his rants into the papers. He hated Tiger Stadium, he said, because it was a home-run park that "the owners can take and throw in the Atlantic Ocean." The Detroit fans were "the biggest front-runners in the world." So what if they booed him last season. "If they think we're stupid for playing this game, how stupid are they for watching us?" "I don't consider myself the best pitcher in the league. I consider myself the best pitcher only on the nights I go out to pitch."

On and on and on. Management didn't like it. But the booing had turned to cheers by the end of May, and the wins just kept on coming.

Ed Sullivan came to the Detroit clubhouse on a trip to Yankee Stadium, and Glen Campbell stopped by in Anaheim.

McLain said he had found a smoke bomb in his wife's car. He said that he had a torn shoulder muscle, but it wasn't serious and he'd go on pitching. In a critical game with Baltimore he started a triple play on a ball lined back to him.

"If I don't catch it, it hits me right in the face," he told reporters. Newspaper photographs showed that he caught the ball near his belt.

Who cares? Keep the carnival rolling.

By early August he passed 20 wins and *Life* magazine assigned a reporter and photographer to follow him full-time. As they rode with him in a cab to Yankee Stadium he rolled down the window at a traffic light and yelled to a woman in the next car, "Hey, honey, want to screw a four-game loser?" That went into the article.

By early September he had won 29 and when he went for his 30th against Oakland at Tiger Stadium, it was Barnum and Bailey and a moon shot all rolled into one. Every major media had a reporter packed into the pressbox. Dizzy Dean showed up to watch Denny tie his record. Sandy Koufax, who had seen a big event or two in his career, was working as a network TV commentator. He just kept shaking his head and saying, "This is unbelievable."

The win didn't come easy. Reggie Jackson hit two homers and the A's led for most of the game. But the Tigers rallied in the ninth and pulled it out when Willie Horton singled over a drawn-in outfield. The picture on the cover of *Sports Illustrated* showed Denny leaping from the dugout, and the arm around him belonged to Al Kaline. Whatever he thought of McLain—and McLain's personality was the diametric opposite of Kaline's—he knew what this moment meant to the team he had played with for so long.

Denny had to come out of the clubhouse for a curtain call. The crowd refused to go home, standing at their seats and chanting his name.

For once, even McLain seemed chastened. He did a complete circle of the stadium perimeter, waving and murmuring, "Thank you."

But he couldn't resist one more visit to the center ring. With the pennant clinched, he went after his 31st against the Yankees. Mickey Mantle came to bat and everyone knew it would be his last appearance in Detroit. He was tied for career home runs with Jimmie Foxx and had struggled to get the one that would break it.

As Mantle came to the plate, the Tigers were ahead by three runs and no one was on base. McLain motioned that he was going to

**DID YOU KNOW . . .** The Tigers were beaten by a highly unlikely relief pitcher at Yankee Stadium in 1968? The short-handed Yankees brought in Rocky Colavito, and when New York rallied to win, the former Detroit right fielder got his one and only big-league win.

# TRIVIA

McLain started 41 times in 1968. How many of those games did he fail to finish?

*Answers to the trivia questions are on page 148.*

throw the ball right down the middle. Mantle, not quite believing what he had seen, fouled it off. McLain made the motion again and Mantle put this pitch into the right-field upper deck. He circled the bases to a standing ovation, with even the rest of the Tigers joining in from their dugout.

It had been one of the wildest rides in Detroit history. McLain finished 31–6. He was signed to play the organ at a postseason date in a hotel on the Vegas Strip, right after he took care of some business in the World Series.

Not many like Denny. That was for sure.

# Christmas in October

He was just the second banana, the lunch bucket guy with the pot-belly and jug ears who showed up to do the best he could.

At one point during the 1968 season, Mickey Lolich was taken out of the rotation for ineffectiveness. He was a streaky pitcher and when he was bad he could be very bad.

On the other hand...

He had been very good at the end of 1967 when the Tigers took the race to the last game of the season. When Denny McLain sagged and succumbed to a mysterious injury, Lolich was the man. He finished only 14–13 but won half of those games in August and September.

Some thought it was his annual stint in the National Guard that held him back. He had to leave for duty two weeks every summer, and while the Detroit riots were going on in July 1967, he was called away to patrol the streets of the city with his unit.

Lolich had been with the Tigers two years longer than McLain and established himself with an 18–9 year in 1964. But he had never again reached that level and was now the definite number two in the rotation.

As the Cardinals prepared for the World Series, however, Roger Maris gave his teammates a scouting report. He had faced both pitchers when he was with the Yankees. He had no doubts that St. Louis could handle McLain. But, he warned, watch out for Lolich.

That wasn't how the Series shaped up in the media or in the minds of most fans. It was to be a historic matchup of 31-game winner McLain and Bob Gibson. The Cardinals ace was the most overpowering pitcher in baseball. He had won nine fewer games than McLain, but 13 of his wins were shutouts, and his ERA was a nearly invisible 1.12.

Lolich wasn't even on the radar screen. He was as down-to-earth and affable as McLain was flighty. Well, he did have a weakness for motorcycles and rode one from his home to the stadium every day. And he did say that he was really a right-hander but only threw lefty

*The play that turned the '68 Series around: Bill Freehan blocks the plate on Lou Brock and then tags him out after snaring Willie Horton's throw from left field. The play gave the Tigers renewed hope, and they would never trail in the Series again.*

**IF ONLY . . .** Dick McAuliffe had hit his hard grounder just a foot or two to the side of Angels' second baseman Bobby Knoop. Knoop was able to start the double play that ended the game and the 1967 season for Detroit. It was the only one McAuliffe hit into all year.

because of a boyhood accident. And he insisted that he really didn't eat all that much, either, because the potbelly was a genetic thing.

Other than that, just one of the guys.

The '68 World Series changed everything. The McLain-Gibson matchup was no contest. Gibson simply swatted away the Tigers like gnats in the Series opener. He struck out 17, setting a record, and the Cards beat McLain easily, 4–0.

Lolich evened it up the next day, 8–1, and hit a home run in the process, the only one of his big-league career.

When the Series returned to Tiger Stadium, however, the Cards really went to work. They took out Earl Wilson in Game 3, 7–3, and with McLain matched against Gibson again in a rainy Game 4, the Tigers were routed, 10–1. This time Gibson hit a homer, too, just to punctuate his superiority.

So it had all been for nothing. Detroit's string of come-from-behind wins during the season. Gates Brown's pinch-hits. McLain's 31. Manager Mayo Smith's incredible gamble of playing his center fielder Mickey Stanley at shortstop to get Al Kaline into the lineup.

None of it mattered. The Cards were just too much. Only two other teams ever had come back from a 3–1 Series deficit, and the Tigers gave no indication that they could compete. Lou Brock was running wild on the bases and, if by some miracle the Tigers did win a couple, Gibson was waiting to put away Game 7.

When Orlando Cepeda slammed a three-run homer off Lolich in the first inning of Game 5, only the truest believers could doubt that it was over.

But those were the last runs the Cardinals would score off Lolich in 16 innings. He started mowing the Redbirds down, and the Tigers started creeping back. By the fifth inning it was 3–2, Cards. Then Brock doubled, and Julian Javier followed with a single to left. This would seal it. The run was almost automatic.

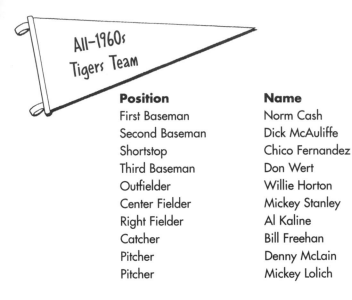

All-1960s
Tigers Team

| Position | Name |
| --- | --- |
| First Baseman | Norm Cash |
| Second Baseman | Dick McAuliffe |
| Shortstop | Chico Fernandez |
| Third Baseman | Don Wert |
| Outfielder | Willie Horton |
| Center Fielder | Mickey Stanley |
| Right Fielder | Al Kaline |
| Catcher | Bill Freehan |
| Pitcher | Denny McLain |
| Pitcher | Mickey Lolich |

Except that Willie Horton was conceding nothing. Regarded as only an adequate fielder, nothing more, Willie charged the ball and threw a strike to Bill Freehan. The catcher, a former football player at the University of Michigan, had the plate sealed off, and when Brock tried to touch it he was bounced to the side. The ball got there at the same instant and Freehan whirled to tag him. Umpire Doug Harvey made the call immediately, and despite Brock's furious protests, he was out and the threat was over.

No one could have known it, but in that instant the Series turned around. Two innings later, Al Kaline looped a two-run single to center and the Tigers had come back, a 5–3 win for Lolich.

Back in St. Louis, they supported McLain with a 12-hit attack, including a grand slam by Jim Northrup, his fifth of the year, to coast home in Game 6, 13–1. So there would be a Game 7 after all. Only the climactic duel would instead be Lolich versus Gibson.

"I slept fine that night," said Lolich. "My biggest concern was getting my family back to Detroit after the game. The seats were all booked on every flight. Once I got that taken care of, there were no worries."

For six innings plus, the two pitchers grappled in a scoreless tie. Fans in two cities watched with clammy hands and tightening viscera.

Not a whisper of a threat. But in the bottom of the sixth Lolich picked two Cards off first, and that seemed to give the Tigers energy.

With two outs in the seventh, Gibson gave up two singles. That brought Northrup to bat, and he sent a sharp liner to center. The ball was hit well, but Curt Flood was one of the best defensive outfielders in the game. The turf was sloppy from a football game played there four days previously, though, and when Flood took a step in on the ball he momentarily lost his footing. The ball cleared his head for a triple. Two runs were in, a third one followed, and the Tigers put it away, 4–1.

"I looked at the left-field stands," said Horton, who scored from second base, "when Fox [Northrup's nickname] hit that ball and I saw Rudolph the Red-Nosed Reindeer coming over the roof."

The celebration in the clubhouse was magnified by a million, 500 miles away in Detroit. Offices emptied as the final out was made on this sunny Thursday afternoon, and the city danced in the streets. Confetti poured down from the skyscrapers, and motorists formed a honking, pennant-waving parade through downtown.

Other fans rushed to the airport, determined to meet the team plane. The field had to be shut down and the Tigers' flight was diverted to another airport. It was an emotional outburst unlike anything Detroit had witnessed since the Tigers of 1935 had won their championship. And like that team, the '68 Tigers remain one of the most beloved groups of athletes in the city's history.

Lolich got a Vegas booking, too, just a few blocks down from where McLain was appearing. He also collected the sports car that went to the outstanding player in the Series.

"I'm a pretty unlikely hero," he said. But in Detroit he was one of the beautiful people.

**DID YOU KNOW . . .** One of Lolich's first endorsement deals with the Tigers was getting to drive a car with the name of a local pizza maker on the side? The sponsor was Mike Ilitch, who bought the team in 1992.

# Billy Ball

The Tigers had a reputation as a buttoned-down, no-nonsense, conservative organization. From owner John Fetzer down, they believed in making the safe choice, the logical decision.

Oh, there were exceptions, such as playing Mickey Stanley at shortstop in the 1968 World Series. But even that didn't compare to hiring Billy Martin as manager three years later. Because if there was anything Martin was not, it was buttoned-down, logical, and safe.

He had twice made his mark previously in Detroit. Once it was as a defensively inadequate shortstop in the 1958 season. The other time was when he managed the Minnesota Twins in 1969 and cold-cocked one of his pitchers in a fight outside the city's best-known sports hangout, the Lindell AC.

That incident normally would have been sufficient to scare the Tigers away from any thought of hiring him. But times were not normal. Two years after winning it all, Mayo Smith was fired. He had lost control of the team and departed with the remark that "Detroit fans wouldn't know a ballplayer from a Japanese aviator." No one was quite sure what that meant, but it sounded bad. Jim Northrup said it a little plainer after that 1970 season. "We just quit on him like dogs."

General manager Jim Campbell was convinced, however, that his veteran team had one more pennant run left in it. The championship nucleus was still intact—with the exception of Denny McLain, who had won a second straight Cy Young Award in 1969 and then toddled off to Weirdsville.

McLain was implicated in a betting scandal before the 1970 season and was suspended by the league for half a year. Upon his return, he celebrated by dumping pails of water over two sportswriters in the

Detroit clubhouse. This time the ballclub suspended him. Then he started complaining of arm problems.

Campbell had enough. He moved Denny to Washington in return for pitcher Joe Coleman Jr. and the whole left side of an infield, shortstop Eddie Brinkman and third baseman Aurelio Rodriguez. It was a steal, reinvigorating the Tigers, while McLain never produced for Washington or anyone else in his short but lively career.

*Unexpected hero Mickey Lolich turned in one of the great clutch performances of all time. His three wins in the 1968 Series stunned St. Louis and brought the Tigers a championship in a historic comeback.*

What was needed, however, was someone who could get the most out of this crew. Enter Mr. Martin.

He had done it with the Twins as a rookie manager, taking them to the Western Division title before losing in the playoffs. That was a team very much like the Tigers, a mix of experienced veterans and a few young stars. After just one season, though, Twins owner Calvin Griffith fired him. Martin fought with nearly everyone in the organization, especially the veteran players. By the end of his tenure he was the most thoroughly hated man in the Minnesota clubhouse.

Still, he'd done the job on the field. Campbell consulted long and hard with his top aide, Hall of Fame catcher Rick Ferrell, and with Fetzer. In the end they decided that the chance to win again outweighed the risk of Martin's abrasive temperament. He got the job in 1971.

Martin had the reputation of being a tough, aggressive player, a quality that endeared him to Yankees manager Casey Stengel. He could use his fists as well as anyone in the game, too, but his fists were wet a lot of the time. He liked to have a drink or few. That habit got him traded from the Yankees and was also responsible for frequent altercations with his own players as a manager.

At first, the dynamic seemed to work in Detroit. The Tigers won 91 games in 1971 and mounted a late run at Baltimore that fell just short. The next year, they took the division.

It was essentially the same team that had won it all, with the addition of the three players acquired for McLain. Not until the last series at Tiger Stadium did they edge out Boston, however, and the path was not smooth.

Martin's position, stated publicly and repeatedly, was that he never made a bad decision in his life, and if things didn't turn out right on the field it had to be the fault of the players. On one occasion, he said he could get better results out of his team by picking a starting lineup out of a hat—which he did. And ended a losing streak in doing it.

None of the Tigers hitters had a good year, and after Lolich and Coleman there wasn't much on the pitching staff. But Al Kaline came back after another of his injuries and got big hits down the stretch, and Woodie Fryman came over in a late deal from the National League and went 10–3. It was just enough. They beat out Boston by a half game in a season shortened at the start by labor problems.

True to Martin's past form, however, the Tigers players despised him. Even as they were winning the division the clubhouse was in a state of near rebellion. Behind his back they accused him of lying to protect his own image.

But with his goading and bullying, they still forced Oakland to the full five games in the playoffs before going out. The front office knew what was happening, but Martin was seen as a hero by the Detroit fans. So they held their nose and brought him back for 1973, and once again he had the team in the thick of the race.

As soon as the Tigers fell out of it in September, however, he was canned. No reason given aside from the usual "differences with management." There were plenty of theories, though.

The players were so fed up they quit on him, as they had on Mayo. He had ruined a promising young left-hander, Les Cain, by forcing him to pitch when he complained of a sore arm. He had made some moves on the daughter of a major team sponsor, who went to Campbell in a fury. His drinking problem was accelerating.

Whatever the reason, and it was probably a combination of all of the above, Martin was gone. Within a few years he would begin his

IF ONLY . . . Umpire John Rice had made an out call on a bang-bang play at first in the fifth game of the 1972 playoffs. First baseman Norm Cash swore for the rest of his life Rice called the runner safe because he hated Billy Martin so much for riding him. The runner came around to score and knocked Detroit out of the playoffs.

psychodrama with Yankees owner George Steinbrenner, who hired and fired him as manager five times.

As for the Tigers, they were placid once again...and began a plummet straight to the cellar. Campbell admitted he probably stayed too long with the players from the championship team because they had accomplished so much for the franchise and the city. Within two years only Lolich, Willie Horton, and Bill Freehan remained.

It was time to begin again.

# The Bird and Friends

With his wild blond curls sticking out from beneath his cap and his loose, long-legged stride, some people thought he looked just like Big Bird, from *Sesame Street*.

So that's what they called Mark Fidrych: "Bird."

And while he won just 29 games in his entire career, he was one of the most adored athletes ever to play in Detroit.

No one ever stole the city's heart the way this gangly 21-year-old kid from Massachusetts did in 1976. Put in the starting rotation in May, in one month he had become the biggest attraction in the game.

He talked to the ball, giving it instructions of what he expected it to do on the way to the plate. Before every inning he went down on his knees and smoothed out the area around the pitcher's rubber like a landscaper. When someone behind him made a good play, he would pump his fist and yell encouragement to his teammate. Once when there was a critical error, he walked over to the player and told him not to worry about it. He'd get the next hitter. And he did.

He was a grown-up kid, someone who brought a simple joy back to a game that was in the first throes of the labor problems that would lead to free agency. Female fans sent cakes and telephone numbers to him in the Tigers clubhouse. Every media outlet in North America wanted to do a story.

"I've got goose bumps," said announcer Bob Prince to a national television audience as Fidrych beat the Yankees at Tiger Stadium. "I've been in this business 30 years and I've got goose bumps."

The sellout crowd was on its feet, screaming "Go, Bird, go" at the top of its lungs as he retired the side in the ninth. The entire country was electrified by the scene.

*Everyone heard about the Bird in 1976. His colorful rookie year made Mark Fidrych a national figure and one of the game's true originals. Injuries cut short his career, but his one shining season still burns bright in Detroit's memory.*

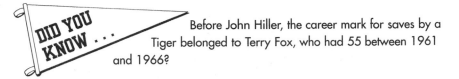

Before John Hiller, the career mark for saves by a Tiger belonged to Terry Fox, who had 55 between 1961 and 1966?

"That young man is the hope of the future for this game," said Calvin Griffith, owner of the Twins.

He was Rookie of the Year, started the All-Star Game, and finished runner-up in the Cy Young Award voting. He finished with a 19–9 record. All this with a team that never had a chance of going anywhere and finished next to last in its division.

These Tigers were a pretty sad bunch. Veteran manager Ralph Houk was brought in to hold things together in a hopeless situation until help could arrive from the farm system. But after a decade of contending teams, the fans had no patience for the product on the field, and attendance was barely clearing one million.

And then came the Bird. He pitched a two-hitter in his starting debut, in which he unveiled all his antics, and as the wins kept coming, so did the fans.

Even Houk, who had managed two world championship teams with the Yankees, was stunned by what he saw. "There is one small area in the strike zone, and if a pitcher can sink a ball there it's almost impossible to hit," he said. "This young man can do it almost every time."

Then came the greatest "if only" in the history of the Tigers. During the next spring training, while horsing around in the outfield at Lakeland, he leaped, came down awkwardly, and damaged his knee. It required surgery, and Fidrych never fully recovered.

He tried coming back several times, and every time he did, the stadium was full again. It seemed at times that he could be the old Bird again. He even pitched a shutout in 1977. But it was always a false hope. His arm would break down every season, and by 1980 he was out of the big leagues for good.

There were other reasons to come out to the ballpark, though. Ron LeFlore was one of them. It was the Gates Brown story all over again. Some youthful misdeeds by the young Detroiter landed him in prison. He'd played some baseball as a kid, and while he was behind bars he went out for the prison team.

## TOP 10

### Wins by a Rookie Pitcher

| | Player | Year | Wins |
|---|---|---|---|
| 1. | Ed Summers | 1908 | 24 |
| 2. | Roscoe Miller | 1901 | 23 |
| 3. | Mark Fidrych | 1976 | 19† |
| | Herman Pillette | 1922 | 19† |
| 5. | Ed Siever | 1901 | 18 |
| 6. | Earl Whitehill | 1924 | 17 |
| 7. | Dave Rozema | 1977 | 15 |
| 8. | Frank Lary | 1955 | 14† |
| | Virgil Trucks | 1942 | 14† |

It turned out he was a natural, with a talent for hitting and the sort of speed that couldn't be taught. Someone at the prison notified the Tigers, and when he finished his time, LeFlore had a tryout and a contract.

He reached the majors in 1974 at the age of 26 and started to run. In less than half a season he stole 23 bases, and in just six years stole 294 of them; that's more than any Detroit player since the end of the dead-ball era. He hit .300 three times, too, and joined Fidrych on the All-Star team in 1976.

But his inexperience showed up in the field, and, more harmfully, in his attitude. When Sparky Anderson took over as manager in 1979, he bristled at LeFlore's casual approach to the game and his apparent willingness to shrug off losses as inconsequential. Given his background that may be understandable, but Sparky was not paid to be a psychologist. LeFlore was dealt to Montreal and in three more years was out of baseball.

The real feel-good story, however, belonged to John Hiller. He had been a member of the '68 champions, splitting his time between starting and long relief. The left-hander seemed intent on enjoying every minute of being a big leaguer and had a reputation for overdoing it a bit in postgame revelry.

While getting in some running at a gym near his Minnesota home before spring training in 1971, he felt severe chest pains. The hospital told him it was a heart attack. He was 28 years old and his career was over.

But not quite. Hiller was determined to make it back. His arm was as strong as ever, and having looked death in the eye his attitude had changed, too. He began a rehabilitation program, gave up the cigarettes and beer, and the following year pleaded with the Tigers to bring him back.

The front office wouldn't hear of it. The risk was too great. But Hiller paid his own way down to Florida, worked out on his own, and lived in the clubhouse at Lakeland because he had no money for lodging. His stamina slowly returned and careful exams by team physicians concluded that he was strong enough to pitch.

He rejoined the Tigers midway through the 1972 season and was a major element in their run to the division title. In 1973 he was the top

## TRIVIA

The 1968 Tigers had two Hall of Famers on their roster. Who were they?

*Answers to the trivia questions are on page 148.*

closer in the league. He saved 38 games, at a time when relievers were not designated as mandatory ninth-inning pitchers. During one stretch, Billy Martin made him stay away from the stadium and disconnect his phone so he wouldn't be tempted to put him in again.

Even as the concept of relief pitching has changed, Hiller still is third on the list of Tigers career saves with 125. He was also the last of the '68 bunch to stay with the team, retiring during the 1980 season.

Not bad for a guy whose career had ended nine years before.

# Tram-aker

They came to the Tigers together and stayed there together, on either side of second base, for the next 19 seasons. They were the most durable double-play team in baseball history, and neither would ever wear another big-league uniform as a player.

Lou Whitaker and Alan Trammell. The shy second baseman from New York City and the talkative shortstop from San Diego. It was an unlikely partnership that formed the base of the resurgent Tigers of the 1980s.

They knew each other's moves, instinctively understood where the other one would be in any situation. It was as if they were one mind in two bodies.

That's why *Sports Illustrated* once referred to them as Tram-aker.

At the end they were just a few points apart in almost every statistic. Trammell hit for a little better average, Whitaker hit for a little more power. Trammell stole a few more bases, Whitaker knocked in a few more runs.

Whitaker finished with 2,369 hits; Trammell with 2,365.

Put all their stats in a milk carton, shake it up, and they would come out homogenized. That's how close they were.

Just on the field, though.

"They put us together the first day in development camp," says Trammell, "and this communication developed. We weren't close friends. It wasn't like that. But we were inside each other's heads.

"There was nothing magical about it. It was work, repetition, over and over again. Sparky [Anderson] always stressed that the definition of a professional is preparation, and if you are not prepared

*Probably the greatest middle infield combo in baseball history, Lou Whitaker and Alan Trammell bid farewell before their final home game together, September 21, 1995. For 18 seasons they thrilled Tigers fans with their uncanny teamwork.*

**All-1970s Tigers Team**

| Position | Name |
|----------|------|
| First Baseman | Jason Thompson |
| Second Baseman | Dick McAuliffe |
| Shortstop | Eddie Brinkman |
| Third Baseman | Aurelio Rodriguez |
| Outfielder | Ron LeFlore |
| Outfielder | Willie Horton |
| Outfielder | Al Kaline |
| Designated Hitter | Rusty Staub |
| Catcher | Bill Freehan |
| Pitcher | Mickey Lolich |
| Pitcher | Joe Coleman Jr. |

for any situation you will be disappointed in your work. The public never saw that part. They just saw Lou throw to the bag without even looking because he knew I was going to be there. That was our advantage, that split second that didn't require a look."

The pair were called up at the end of the 1977 season, another desultory year of wandering around the second division of the American League East. It was Detroit's fourth straight year below .500.

Maybe it was coincidence. Maybe it was a confluence of several other factors. But when Tram-aker moved into the starting lineup the next spring, the Tigers did not have another losing season for the next 11 years. They were both 20 years old.

There was never a doubt about their defense. Almost immediately Whitaker was recognized as the best-fielding second baseman in the league. Trammell wasn't far behind among shortstops.

But it appeared they would be pinch-hitters for most of their careers. Whitaker's speed put him at the leadoff spot in the lineup while Trammell hit seventh. The two of them combined for a total of just 31 home runs in their first four seasons in the majors.

Then something clicked. Gates Brown, who was then the team's hitting coach, said it was simply a matter of getting them to turn on the ball. Or maybe it was a matter of maturity, of filling out and getting stronger.

Whatever the explanation, from 1982 on they were offensive weapons with dangerous extra-base power. Whitaker's career total of 244 home runs is sixth best in Tigers history. Trammell hit 28 dingers and 105 RBIs in the 1987 season, when the Tigers won the divisional title. He probably should have been voted the league's MVP, but lost out to Toronto's George Bell.

The other thing that happened was that Trammell became the leader of the team. This was important because it was a position that had gone unfilled for many years. There had been no one to set the tone, demand accountability. Trammell stepped into the role.

"There were a lot of tough guys in that clubhouse," recalled first baseman Dave Bergman. "Kirk Gibson, Jack Morris. Tram wouldn't hesitate to get in the face of any of them. That's because everyone just respected him so much."

"I watched him do it with Lance Parrish, who was one of the strongest men I'd ever seen in the big leagues," said Sparky Anderson. "And I'd say to myself, 'Better be careful there. He can twist you up like a pretzel.' But Trammell being Trammell, he could get away with it."

The one guy who never came in for any of his needling was Whitaker.

"I knew him too well," Trammell explained.

Many years later, when Trammell was named manager of the Tigers, one of his first actions was to call Whitaker and invite him to spring training as a coach. Whitaker made his home in Lakeland but felt the team had moved on and forgotten about him. Retiring as ever, he didn't feel it was his place to make an approach. So he simply stayed away from training camp.

By the NUMBERS

**308**—Mickey Lolich's strikeout total in 1971, highest in team history.

Trammell understood. He didn't even need to look. Just like always.

Besides this combination, the Tigers' long-term strategy seemed to be working. After a long drought, the farm system was producing again. Parrish would become a power-hitting catcher with the best arm in the league. Morris and Dan Petry would anchor the pitching staff. Tom Brookens would take over at third, and Gibson gradually moved into a starting job in the outfield.

By 1981, the year that baseball conjured up a split season because of a players' strike, the Tigers startled everyone by making a serious run at the Eastern Division title in the second half.

They weren't quite ready yet, though, and fell short. But Tiger Stadium was awake and alive once more.

# Sparky's Way

If you went to draw a picture of how a big-league manager should look, it probably would come out bearing a strong resemblance to Sparky Anderson.

If ever a man looked the part it was Sparky. He was just 36 years old when he was first named manager at Cincinnati and he already appeared as if he'd been through the wars. Gray hair, lined face, and an air of command that brooked no opposition.

"My way or the highway" was more than just an idle slogan with him. If you didn't buy into the program, you worked somewhere else.

"I never cared if they liked me," he said. "I wasn't there to be their friend. Some managers make that mistake. But that wasn't my job. I was there to put them in a position where they had a chance to succeed. If they didn't understand, that made it very easy for me. They were sitting ducks."

When he was named to manage the Tigers in June 1979, it was hardly surprising. He had won four pennants and two championships with the Reds, but when he was unceremoniously dumped by them at the end of the previous season it qualified as a shocker.

So when Sparky got the call from the Tigers the following June, it made sense. It was just the timing that was a bit off.

At the time Sparky was pink-slipped, Detroit already had committed to Les Moss as their new manager for 1979. The team seemed poised to do great things and Moss, an old and steady baseball hand, was a safe choice. True, he had never been a full-time manager before. But after the turmoil of the Billy Martin episode earlier in the 1970s, the front office viewed safe as a great quality.

The Tigers run the second-oldest and most successful fantasy camp in baseball? It has been operating since 1984 and is the only such camp where demand is so high that two one-week sessions are run each winter at Lakeland.

The Tigers were one game over .500 when Moss was shown the door. It wasn't a terrible performance. But general manager Jim Campbell had learned that Sparky was through pouting over his dismissal and ready to start managing again. And other teams were interested.

"Les was doing a good job but a talent like Sparky doesn't come along every day," said Campbell by way of explanation.

The move was not immediately popular among the Tigers. Moss was a fatherly type and Anderson, decidedly, was not.

Pitcher Milt Wilcox, who had played for him in Cincinnati, knew what to expect. "Young players could get in his doghouse without ever knowing why," he said. "It happened to me and there was no reason. He just liked veterans."

It wasn't an altogether fair rap. Sparky did inherit a bunch of big-time stars in Cincinnati—Pete Rose, Johnny Bench, Tony Perez. But he also brought along younger players such as Dave Concepcion, Ken Griffey, and Don Gullett. Still, there were those who regarded him as a push-button manager who had simply lucked into one of the greatest teams of all time.

There were no established stars on the Tigers of 1979. But there were a bunch of players with a lot of promise. Even more than in his days with the Big Red Machine, this was going to be Sparky's team, the chance to show the jokers that there was more to him than buttons.

He started out by building them up. Jack Morris was "the best right-handed pitcher in the American League," said Sparky, although he clearly was not. At least, not yet. Kirk Gibson had a chance to be "the next Mickey Mantle." Any number of young players whose names are now all but forgotten were "can't-miss prospects."

Sparky excelled at the old confidence game.

On the other hand, Rusty Staub was gone almost immediately and Ron LeFlore followed soon afterward. They had been big producers in Detroit and both were veterans, but they had attitude problems. At least, they did with Sparky.

Two of the bright young stars of the farm system, Jason Thompson and Steve Kemp, also were bade good-bye. They still had productive years in their futures. Only not in Detroit.

Meanwhile, the team continued to bob up and down, stuck between 83 and 85 wins a year—aside from the strike-shortened 1981 campaign.

*When Sparky Anderson said, "My way or the highway," he wasn't kidding. He could be ornery, but his players learned to respect his methods, and he led them to the 1984 World Championship.*

# TOP 10

## Wins for Tigers Managers

| | Manager | Years | Wins |
|---|---|---|---|
| 1. | Sparky Anderson | 1979–95 | 1,331 |
| 2. | Hughie Jennings | 1907–20 | 1,131 |
| 3. | Bucky Harris | 1929–33, 1955–56 | 516 |
| 4. | Steve O'Neill | 1943–48 | 509 |
| 5. | Ty Cobb | 1921–26 | 479 |
| 6. | Del Baker | 1933, 1938–42 | 417 |
| 7. | Mayo Smith | 1967–70 | 363† |
| | Ralph Houk | 1974–78 | 363† |
| 9. | Mickey Cochrane | 1934–38 | 348 |
| 10. | Red Rolfe | 1949–52 | 278 |

This wasn't the kind of progress that had been anticipated. But trust in Sparky remained unabated. After all, he had to know what he was doing.

"He'll change his mind about a player five times between the time he leaves the stadium to when he gets home," said Campbell. "But that's what makes Sparky go."

The media loved him. Sparky could always be counted on to say something like, "Pain don't hurt." Things that almost made sense if you thought about them for a while.

He always had something good, a news nugget or a quote, for his beat writers. He was a great interview when the national media showed up. He knew how to keep his fences mended.

"My daddy always used to say that it don't cost nothin' to be nice to people," he said. "The biggest mistake people make is when they bad-mouth people. Once you bad-mouth people you can't take it back."

He was fundamentally a decent and kind man, and that shone through. If he was sometimes called Captain Hook because of the way he'd yank his pitchers out of a game if they even got a wild look in their eyes, it was nothing personal. At least, not to him.

Like most managers, Sparky believed that winning teams must be strong up the middle. By 1982 the Tigers were finally there. Lance Parrish, Alan Trammell, Lou Whitaker, the pitching staff—all as good as it gets.

When he traded for Chet Lemon as his center fielder, an outstanding defensive player who could hit, all the pieces were finally in place.

In 1983 the Tigers broke out of their rut, won 92 games, and were on Baltimore's heels well into September. It was the most games the team had won since the 1968 championship.

Now they were more than poised for success. They were ready to make the leap.

# 1984 and *The Natural*

Some of the Tigers thought of it as a fulfillment of their sports fantasy when they were growing up.

"We knew we were going to go out there every day and beat you," said pitcher Dan Petry. "And the next day we were going to do it again. That's the greatest feeling there is."

"All I knew is that we were making history and I was a part of it," said designated hitter Darrell Evans. "I just wanted to enjoy the ride."

To Tigers fans, however, it was something even more. It was like an out-of-body experience. There had been so many disappointments, so many close calls over the years. Sometimes they believed the team's motto should be: "Let's almost win."

To start the 1984 season by going 35–5—well, words were inadequate. One of the big Hollywood releases that spring was a baseball film with Robert Redford, *The Natural*. In Detroit it was as if their team had suddenly grown a dugout full of Naturals.

"Bless you, boys," which had been introduced as an ironic statement by local sportscaster Al Ackerman a few years before, became the catchphrase. The Wave encircled the old ballpark in joyful celebration.

The only man who wasn't swept up in the euphoria was Sparky Anderson. As the wins mounted to an unreal level, Sparky began to fret.

"I kept thinking that if we lose this thing now they'll come and hang me," he said. "And they would have every right to."

Jack Morris pitched a no-hitter on the first weekend of the season and that seemed to set the tone. Nothing was impossible.

If Sparky needed a little thunder from the bench he simply sent in Dave Bergman or Rusty Kuntz. Who were they? It didn't matter. They got the hits.

*Willie Hernandez nails down the last out of the '84 Series and is mobbed by his teammates, led by catcher Lance Parrish. With a 35–5 start, the team was in first place from Opening Day to the end of the season.*

TIGERS ESSENTIAL

**By the NUMBERS**

**10-10**—Jack Morris's record in 1984 after the 35–5 start.

If he needed late-inning help, he motioned for Willie Hernandez. The left-handed screwballer was almost perfect all year long, saved 32 games, and wound up as the league's MVP and Cy Young Award winner.

"I had years when I threw the ball harder," he said. "But I never had the location like that again. I knew I could put the ball right where I wanted."

On days when Hernandez was indisposed, or when a set-up man was required, Sparky turned to Aurelio Lopez. He had been moved out of the closer role by Hernandez, but he was still Señor Smoke, with a fastball that could be overpowering. He saved 14 and won 10 more, and only in later years did he bridle at the perceived drop in bullpen status.

The Tigers had demonstrated serious intent this season by acquiring their first major free agent in Evans. Conservative as always, Detroit had treated free agency with all the enthusiasm of finding a cobra in their dugout. "Build from within" was the organization's mantra.

But now they were so close, and Evans was such a good fit for the short right-field fence in Tiger Stadium.

"I was in town that winter before I really had made up my mind on who to sign with," he said, "and they took me to a hockey game. They announced that I was there and the crowd stood up and gave me an ovation. I hadn't even signed with Detroit and that's how I was being welcomed. That clinched it for me."

When Toronto made a run at the Tigers in June, the team called up Ruppert Jones from the minors. A former All-Star center fielder, he had been sitting around without a contract that spring when the Tigers offered him a minor league assignment. Two days after being summoned, he crushed a three-run homer that deflated the Blue Jays.

It was simply that kind of year.

After the blazing start, Detroit was 69–53 the rest of the way and was never seriously threatened. They finished first by 15 games and won a franchise record 104.

They never relaxed. With people like Morris and Gibson in the clubhouse, no one dared to relax.

"They were ornery bastards," said Sparky. "Nothing wrong with that. I liked a few ornery bastards on my team. I was kind of one myself."

For Gibson, the vast promise was finally realized. He had been an All-American end at Michigan State. Had he pursued football, and he was a first-round draft pick, few doubted he would have been a star in the NFL. Baseball had been a second choice in college, but it was the path that promised greater longevity. It wasn't the easier path for Gibson, but he didn't prefer easy.

"I had a few attitude problems," he says. "I'd go into a situation and say, 'You want to race me, I can beat you. You want to tackle me, I'll knock the shit out of you.' But baseball is a game where you have to defeat your inner doubts more than anything else, and that came harder for me."

Sparky had brought along his potential superstar slowly. Injuries also held him back. Not until 1983, his fourth year with the team, was he a regular, and it was a disaster. He hit just .227 and seemed bewildered much of the time.

During the off-season he dropped from sight and went to the Pacific Institute in Seattle. He learned how to grapple with what he called the Beast, the doubts that were holding back his positive energy. He came back with a changed outlook.

"I not only was comfortable with my role as a ballplayer, I was comfortable with my role in life," he said.

Gibson, more than any other individual, was the rock of the 1984 season. The Natural had arrived at last.

The Tigers led the race from the first day to the last, wire to wire, the first team since the 1927 Yankees to do that. Kansas City swept a four-game series in August and that gave the Royals hope going into the

## TRIVIA

A record by a Motown artist, who later was elected to political office in Detroit, became the team's unofficial theme song, played at every home game during the 1984 season. What was it?

*Answers to the trivia questions are on page 148.*

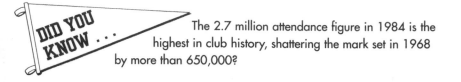

playoffs, but Detroit brushed them away in a three-game sweep of their own.

Then it was the World Series and San Diego. The Padres managed to win just once, and in four of the five games their starter couldn't get past the third inning.

Fittingly, it was Gibson who brought it all home. His three-run homer off Goose Gossage at a delirious Tiger Stadium in Game 5 clinched it. The photograph of him, both fists raised in the air, bellowing in triumph as he returned to the dugout, his uniform pants torn from an earlier slide home, became the emblem of this remarkable year. They didn't have to come and hang Sparky. Instead it was copies of this picture, taken by *Detroit Free Press* photographer Mary Schroeder, that was hung on home and office walls all over Michigan for many years afterward.

For an entire generation it was the essence of baseball in Detroit.

# Pizza Wars

For most of the 20th century, the Detroit Tigers had been run by three men: Frank Navin, Walter Briggs, and John Fetzer.

Responsible, conservative, and committed to operating the ball-club as a public trust, they brought a remarkable sense of continuity to the franchise and, as a result, Detroit was one of the most profitable teams in baseball.

Fetzer, a broadcast executive, also wielded an enormous amount of influence among other owners because he showed them how to unlock the honey pot and get more money for their television rights than they ever dreamed possible.

But after 22 years of running the Tigers, Fetzer was beginning to look for a successor. He thought he found one in Tom Monaghan, who had grown a single store in the college town of Ypsilanti, Michigan, into a national pizza powerhouse. His big idea was developing a way to deliver cheap, hot pizzas to students. It made him a fortune.

Monaghan, who grew up in an orphanage, was also an ardent Tigers fan. He credited baseball and the team with giving a focus to his life.

When he first approached Fetzer about buying the Tigers in 1983, the older man said he wasn't interested. But upon reflection he thought that maybe the time and situation were right. Monaghan was local, loved baseball, and appeared willing to carry on in the same tradition. So in 1984 Monaghan, rookie owner and adoring fan, found himself with a championship. Things went downhill from there.

*The Tigers plucked Cecil Fielder from obscurity in Japan, and he responded with a 51-home-run season in 1991. The big first baseman was a perennial long-ball threat for a noncontending ballclub.*

**IF ONLY . . .** The Tigers had been a little more farsighted in getting Doyle Alexander from the Braves in 1987. Alexander helped secure the division title in that one year. But in return Atlanta received John Smoltz, one of the top pitchers of the next 20 years.

Monaghan was a man of many enthusiasms. A devout Catholic, he wanted to restore historic cathedrals in Central America. He was a student of Frank Lloyd Wright and wanted to build things in homage to Wright's architectural ideals. He embarked on a scheme to create a destination golf resort on remote Drummond Island, in Michigan's Upper Peninsula.

All these things cost money, and Jim Campbell, now the team's president, found the budget for the ballclub static in the face of rising free-agency prices. Lance Parrish was the first to depart for a bigger payday, followed by Kirk Gibson and Jack Morris. Making it worse, funds were being diverted from the farm system, the team's traditional font of talent.

There was still enough talent on hand to win the division title in 1987, wresting it away from Toronto on the season's final day. But the Twins upset them in the playoffs, and a slow, inexorable decline was under way. Tiger Stadium had seen the last postseason game in its history.

In 1989 the team lost 103 games and Sparky Anderson had to take a leave from the ballclub for undisclosed reasons. Over the next 16 years, there would only be two winning seasons, and no serious run at the playoffs.

One of the proudest franchises in baseball was in tatters. The fans put the blame squarely on Monaghan. He went from an object of admiration—the poor but hardworking youth who was living the dream—to one of ridicule.

The organization was convinced what it needed most was a new ballpark. Maintenance costs at Tiger Stadium were soaring, the fan base was moving to the suburbs, and almost every game was now being televised. Obviously the folks wanted something new and exciting to bring them back.

All-1980s
Tigers Team

| Position | Name |
| --- | --- |
| First Baseman | Darrell Evans |
| Second Baseman | Lou Whitaker |
| Shortstop | Alan Trammell |
| Third Baseman | Tom Brookens |
| Outfielder | Larry Herndon |
| Outfielder | Chet Lemon |
| Outfielder | Kirk Gibson |
| Catcher | Lance Parrish |
| Designated Hitter | Johnny Grubb |
| Pitcher | Jack Morris |
| Pitcher | Dan Petry |

Monaghan thought he knew the answer. Bo Schembechler had stepped down as football coach at Michigan and was now athletics director. Here was a man who could get things done, and a hero besides. Monaghan placed him in charge of the baseball operation with job one of getting the new stadium built.

But Schembechler was out of his element. He wasn't dealing with college kids on scholarships anymore. His statement that "you cannot chain us to a rusty girder" infuriated both those who wanted to preserve the ballpark and the politicians who felt they were being unduly pressured to pay for a new one. When Bo appeared to acquiesce to the firing of popular announcer Ernie Harwell, he was pilloried.

In 1992, with the entire front office in Cooperstown to watch Hal Newhouser's induction into the Hall of Fame, Monaghan dropped the bomb. He sold the club to his bitter pizza rival, Mike Ilitch, owner of Little Caesar's.

Campbell, who had devoted his entire career to the Tigers, was fired by long-distance telephone. So was Schembechler, who ended up suing Monaghan. Most of the front-office staff followed them out the door.

For Ilitch, too, it was the culmination of a dream. He, too, had started with just one pizza store and built an empire. He had been a decent minor league ballplayer once. Not quite good enough to make the Tigers but now rich enough to own them.

"When I was growing up in Detroit," he said at the introductory ceremony at the ballpark, "the Tigers were discussed around every dinner table in the city every evening. I want to make sure that happens again."

He succeeded, but not quite in the way he intended. The first order of business was signing Cecil Fielder. The hulking first baseman had come out of nowhere—well, it was Japan, actually—to hit 51 homers for the Tigers in 1990. Only Hank Greenberg had ever hit more in one season for Detroit. Fielder was an immediate star and the team's sole gate attraction.

He was given a five-year, $36 million deal. It was not only the highest in Detroit history but also made Fielder the best-paid player in the majors. It also drained the team's budget, making it impossible for them to compete in the free-agent market. When attendance continued its decline, the Tigers were trapped in a vicious circle. If people discussed the Tigers at dinner at all, it was not happy talk.

The 1994 lockout seemed to strip the last bit of fan sympathy from the operation in this strong union town. Sparky left the following year and attendance went down to 1.1 million—near the bottom of all franchises in the major leagues.

Fielder was dealt to the Yankees, but the team still couldn't afford to pay its All-Star third baseman, Travis Fryman, who was allowed to leave as a free agent. Sports radio bristled with indignation, and the columnists had a fit.

In another part of Ilitch's sports domain, the Red Wings were winning back-to-back Stanley Cups in 1997 and 1998. The Wings were the talk of the town, not the Tigers. All they got were the sounds of silence and a vast cavern of empty seats.

# Good-Bye to the Corner

When it became apparent that the threat to Tiger Stadium was real, a group of devotees gathered on the corner of Michigan and Trumbull avenues one day.

After pointing out that a century's worth of baseball had been played on this site, they turned to the ballpark and gave it a hug. Their line stretched around the corner, to the street once called National but renamed Cochrane. In the other direction, it extended to the street once called Cherry but renamed Kaline.

They may have said they were hugging the stadium. In reality, though, they were embracing their memories, trying to gather them close before they were sealed away.

Thousands and thousands of summer afternoons and evenings. Sitting in these stands with the people who mattered most in their lives. Parents and grandparents. Children and spouses. Siblings and friends.

Hug them as if you never wanted to let them go.

A group calling itself the Tiger Stadium Fan Club presented a professionally drawn-up proposal for a remodeling that would have provided private boxes and a few other amenities Tigers ownership said were needed.

They were smiled at politely and brushed off. That wasn't going to happen. It had to be a new stadium. The only question was whether it would be built within the city of Detroit or go to the suburbs.

The majority of fans seemed to understand. Or maybe they were just inured to it by the long string of losing seasons. The 1991 Tigers, led by Cecil Fielder, had actually been in the pennant race into

August before their shortage in pitching ended the run. Since then, a big zippo.

So if a new ballpark could make Detroit a competitive franchise again, let it be.

There did seem to be promise. The farm system once more was sending up players. Tony Clark was a genuine power threat at first. Outfielders Gabe Kapler and Juan Encarnacion had been minor league superstars. Justin Thompson, Jeff Weaver, and Brian Moehler gave them a solid core of starters, and this Matt Anderson kid could throw triple-digit fastballs in relief.

A new ballpark would mean higher attendance, it was argued, and that would translate into more money to get the free agents who would fill in the gaps on this team. Maybe it really was time to say good-bye.

*The heroes of the past return to their field of dreams in 1999 at Tiger Stadium's final curtain call. After spending its entire existence at the corner of Michigan and Trumbull, the ballclub looked forward to a new beginning.*

| Position | Name |
|---|---|
| First Baseman | Tony Clark |
| Second Baseman | Damion Easley |
| Shortstop | Alan Trammell |
| Third Baseman | Travis Fryman |
| Outfielder | Bobby Higginson |
| Outfielder | Tony Phillips |
| Outfielder | Kirk Gibson |
| Catcher | Mickey Tettleton |
| Designated Hitter | Cecil Fielder |
| Pitcher | Justin Thompson |
| Pitcher | Todd Jones |

The Fan Club didn't go quietly. Its membership was earnest, media savvy, and had some legal smarts, too. But there was just too much establishment weight lined up against them and they lost an unequal battle.

And now it was September 1999. As the old song about this month says, the days had dwindled down to a precious few.

The fans had turned out all through the season, making special trips with old friends and family, to say their farewells. For the first year since 1988, when the team was still regarded as a contender, attendance topped 2 million. Someone suggested that with those numbers they should have announced a closing every year.

The announced attendance for the finale was 43,000 and change, an indication of how capacity had shrunk over the years. Sections had been closed off, obstructed-view seats weren't sold. At the end, it wasn't much bigger than Navin Field had been in 1937.

It was a magnificent late-summer afternoon, and when Robert Fick, one of those promising young players, smashed a grand slam off the facing of the third deck in right, the place went up for grabs. Here, as if scripted, was the final memory for the Corner.

Then it was time.

They had gathered in the old bullpen area, beneath the center-field bleachers, and one by one they came trotting out to the positions they once played on this turf.

Here was Elden Auker, 89 years old, one of the last living members of the 1935 champions, driven out in a golf cart. Auker passed away in 2006.

And Mark Fidrych, the Bird, sprinting out to the mound as if he were 21 again and it was 1976 with the world at his fingertips. He went to his hands and knees and began smoothing out the area. Just like yesterday.

Here was Willie Horton moving to his old familiar place in left. A few days before, Willie had said he didn't know whether he'd be able to do this. The emotions might be too much for him. But he had gathered himself, and there he was, a little heavier, but still and always the kid who had come off the streets of the city to stardom.

Here was Ron LeFlore, a lot heavier, moving into center. The base-stealing speed of his playing days was long gone. He hadn't been back in Detroit for several years, and with good reason. Right after the closing ceremony he was arrested for nonpayment of child support.

# TRIVIA

**Only one Detroit pitcher won 20 games in a season during the 1990s. Who was he?**

*Answers to the trivia questions are on page 148.*

Here was Jim Bunning, now a U.S. Senator from Kentucky. Tiger Stadium crowds traditionally booed the politicians who tried to hog the spotlight on Opening Day. But there was nothing but cheers for Bunning at closing day.

Here was Eddie Mayo, sparkplug of the 1945 champions, making his way slowly to second base. He hadn't even been called until a few days before. The assumption was he would be too frail or uninterested. But he came, too.

Here was Al Kaline, trotting out to the right field he had graced for all those years.

Here were Alan Trammell and Lou Whitaker, running onto the field together, side by side as they always had been, until they reached second base, and then parted ways to take their old positions.

DID YOU KNOW . . . Tony Clark set the club record for home runs in a season by a switch-hitter with 34 in 1998?

So many tears. A father tried to explain to his young son why he stood up and cheered when Mickey Lolich came on the field, and he couldn't continue. He just shook his head as the tears rolled down his cheeks.

On and on they came. The protocol was well established. All the old ballparks were closing down and had said similar good-byes. Only Fenway and Wrigley were left from this era, but Tiger Stadium had been older than either of them.

Auker spoke for the rest of them, thanking the Detroit fans for all their support through the years and speaking about what it meant to play for this team.

Home plate was dislodged and carried to the new stadium, still under construction a mile to the east. The center-field flagpole would follow in time.

The ceremony wrapped up. The lights went out. And it was over.

# New Century, New Home

A few days before the first Opening Day at Comerica Park, Al Kaline and Willie Horton stood at home plate of the new stadium and looked out at left field.

Neither one of them said a word for a minute. Finally, Kaline broke the silence.

"Awful long way out there, Will," he said.

One might think that if these guys, the first and fourth most prolific home-run hitters in Tigers history, thought the fences were too distant, it was a pretty good indication that something had gone terribly wrong.

Detroit's new ballpark opened for the 2000 season with a rush of enthusiasm. There were many things to admire about it. It was located in the middle of downtown and seemed to herald a rebirth of the urban core. It was open in right field and looked out upon a dramatic view of the Detroit skyline. One could walk around the entire stadium without a barrier, which was impossible at Tiger Stadium. Poster displays and a row of statues behind the center-field wall celebrating the great players of the past gave it a firm link with the team's history. A Ferris wheel. A picnic area. A fountain in center. All quite wonderful.

At times it seemed, though, as if the Tigers had built a magnificent stadium but forgotten that it was supposed to be a ballpark.

The sense of intimacy, the feeling of hanging right over the field in the upper deck, was gone. The pitch of the field-level seats was too low, making for bad sight lines. And the distances were forbidding, as Kaline pointed out. It was 402 feet to the left-field power alley and 379 to the one in right.

Not only was that absurdly long, it completely reversed the sort of baseball the Tigers had played in the past. This was a team that thrived on the long ball and a little pitching. But in this stadium, they had to unplug the power and bring on the arms.

The Tigers front office said to look on the park as a work in progress. Besides, they didn't want to build yet another home-run gallery with a retro look. They wanted a distinctly different approach from the other new ballparks.

They certainly succeeded in that. But there was a much bigger problem to deal with. Because although the ballpark's address may have changed, the Tigers were still bad and getting worse.

In late 1999 the Tigers swung their biggest deal in years. Unfortunately, they paid for it almost immediately. They obtained Juan Gonzalez, one of the top sluggers in the league, from Texas. But

*Opening Day number one at Comerica Park. The new stadium got mixed reviews from fans and media, but it did open up on spectacular views of the city's skyline and promised to restore some life to downtown.*

**DID YOU KNOW . . .** The Tigers chose one of their top prospects, pitcher Francisco Cordero, for the symbolic act of carrying home plate to Comerica Park from Tiger Stadium at the old park's closing ceremonies? Two months later he was sent to Texas in the Juan Gonzalez deal.

they traded away three of the young prospects upon whom they were ostensibly building their future.

Moreover, Gonzalez was known to be a bit of a crankypuss. When he looked at the same view that Kaline and Horton had seen, he pitched a fit. He had averaged 37 homers over the previous nine years. It didn't take him long to figure out he wasn't going to come anywhere close to that in this canyon of a ballpark.

He finished with just 22, missed a lot of time with injuries, and cursed the ballpark to the media on a regular basis. He also became the first player to be booed regularly at Comerica, and when he came back the following season in a Cleveland uniform he was booed even more.

The trade to get him had made no sense on the face of it. The Tigers needed players who fit their new home: line-drive hitters, defensive whizzes, pitchers. The last thing they needed was a slow long-ball hitter.

The club eventually brought in that left-center fence by 32 feet and shortened the one in right by 14 feet. It made a difference in the aesthetics of the game, but the team was still horrid.

In the first three years at Comerica they were 85 games under .500. Then things really got bad.

Dave Dombrowski, who had put together a winner in Florida in just five years, the fastest pace ever for an expansion team, was hired as general manager to try to straighten out the mess. He understood that the club had to be torn down completely in order to begin again, and it was not going to be pretty. So one of the old heroes, Alan Trammell, was hired as manager to deflect the outrage.

Trammell knew what he was in for and tried hard. But he was an inexperienced manager and it was an impossible task. He had played on some bad teams in Detroit, but the 2003 Tigers were beyond bad. Their record of 43–119 was not only the worst in team history, it also

**386–585**—Detroit's record in the first six years they played at Comerica Park.

came within one loss of equaling the record for futility set by the 1962 Mets. Only a three-game final-weekend sweep of a Minnesota team that already had clinched its playoff spot and was coasting avoided that dubious achievement.

Mike Maroth went 9–21, the first big-league pitcher to lose 20 since 1980. As an indication of how bad things were, he had the best winning percentage among the starters. Jeremy Bonderman, in only his second year of professional baseball, was 6–19. The Tigers hoped the experience would speed the maturation of their young pitchers, and not their demoralization.

Dmitri Young had a semblance of a season, hitting 29 homers and 85 RBIs. The numbers are all the more remarkable because there was no one else in the lineup to concern opposing pitchers.

Trammell had brought in some teammates from the 1984 champions—Kirk Gibson and Lance Parrish—as coaches. They knew how to win. It seemed, however, they were the only three guys in the clubhouse who did.

Worse yet, after the initial attendance spurt created by curiosity about the new ballpark, the figures were dropping again. In this abysmal 2003 season, they were right where they were when the decision was made that Tiger Stadium was no longer tenable.

The Ferris wheel and picnic area and view of the skyline could not take the place of a winning team. Owner Mike Ilitch had promised that when the Tigers got close he would open up the vault and pay for players who could turn them into winners again.

It hadn't happened yet. There were no good memories at Comerica Park. Just the steady drip of failure.

# Welcome to the Future

Four months after finishing a season that was more like a waking nightmare, something astonishing happened to the Tigers. They convinced Pudge Rodriguez to come and play in their yard.

It isn't always easy to pinpoint exactly when a long run of sorrowful luck suddenly turns itself around. But in this case it was a cinch: February 4, 2004. The difficult thing is figuring out why.

Rodriguez, a catcher headed for the Hall of Fame, was just coming off a championship season with the Florida Marlins. He was a highly prized commodity in the free-agent market.

And there he was sitting beside Alan Trammell, who looked like a man who opened his sock drawer one day and found a winning lottery ticket. It was not only that Rodriguez was the most important free agent ever to sign with the Tigers. It was that it came when the franchise was at the lowest ebb in its long history.

Detroit was desperate for something that would restore its credibility, anything that would halt its sickening descent into baseball oblivion. Rodriguez was the answer to their prayers. He said he liked a challenge, and he had just landed up to his neck in one.

Rodriguez said all the right things, smiled for the cameras, and then went out and had an All-Star season. He hit .334 and handled the young pitching staff with a master's hands.

But Dave Dombrowski wasn't finished. Having pulled a superstar out of the hat, he went and levitated a power-hitting shortstop from out of nowhere. Carlos Guillen came from Seattle in a fairly unheralded trade with a reputation as a good defensive player who didn't hit much. He proceeded to bat .318 and knocked in 97 runs.

Brandon Inge, moved out as the regular catcher by Rodriguez, tacked 80 points onto his batting average as a starting third baseman. Craig Monroe became a solid everyday player in left. At the end of the year, the Tigers had improved by 29 games and were closing in on respectability.

When Magglio Ordoñez signed as another major free-agent pickup in 2005, it seemed the Tigers were almost there and picking up steam.

Funny how things work out, though. With everybody talking playoffs, Ordoñez and Guillen went down with injuries for much of the season. Rodriguez went into a funk and fell out with Trammell.

*The biggest free-agent signing in the team's history brought Pudge Rodriguez to town in 2004, following the worst season in Tigers history. The catcher symbolized the rebirth of baseball spirit in 2006 as a winning team returned to Detroit.*

**.222**—Jim Leyland's lifetime batting average in the minors.

Troy Percival, picked up to be the closer, was ineffective and then tore a muscle that ended his career. The team never was in the race. It even fell back a game from its modest win total of 2004.

The fans had expected much, much more. Trammell, who had been a good soldier when conditions were hopeless, bore the brunt of their anger now. He was fired at the end of the season, reduced in rank to ex-hero.

It was the 11th year in a row below .500 for the forlorn franchise. An entire generation of youngsters had grown up in Detroit without ever seeing their team in a pennant race. Many of them had taken to wearing Red Sox or Yankees caps and cheering for those teams when they came to town.

Forty-two years before this sad state of affairs, the Tigers had signed a young catcher from Toledo to a minor league contract. He kicked around in their farm system for seven years, never even making it up to the big club for the proverbial cup of coffee. Finally Jim Leyland had to face facts. At the age of 26 he took off the mask and shin guards and became a manager.

He developed a reputation for handling difficult young players. Kirk Gibson credits Leyland with transforming him from a college hotshot into a professional ballplayer. "He threatened to send me home if I didn't, no matter how big a contract I had, and I believe he would have," said Gibson.

Just as he seemed ready to get a shot with the Tigers, however, the big club hired Sparky Anderson. Leyland knew his way to the manager's chair was blocked, and he left the organization. Subsequently, he took Pittsburgh to three divisional titles. Then he was hired by Dombrowski in Florida and led the Marlins to their first championship in 1997. Two years later, though, he went to Colorado, had a terrible season, and announced his retirement. He said the competitive fires had gone out.

Now they were burning again and he was ready to take another shot. He had finally made it to Detroit. A little late but set to go. Just

**TOP 10**

Games Played for the Tigers, Career

| | Player | Games Played | Years |
|---|---|---|---|
| 1. | Al Kaline | 2,834 | 1953–74 |
| 2. | Ty Cobb | 2,805 | 1905–26 |
| 3. | Lou Whitaker | 2,390 | 1977–95 |
| 4. | Charlie Gehringer | 2,323 | 1924–42 |
| 5. | Alan Trammell | 2,293 | 1977–96 |
| 6. | Sam Crawford | 2,114 | 1903–17 |
| 7. | Norm Cash | 2,018 | 1960–74 |
| 8. | Harry Heilmann | 1,989 | 1914, 1916–29 |
| 9. | Donie Bush | 1,872 | 1908–21 |
| 10. | Bill Freehan | 1,774 | 1961, 1963–76 |

like owner Mike Ilitch, another one-time bust in the minors, Leyland had simply arrived by a slightly longer route.

He was 61 years old, gray-haired, with a face that showed the effects of too many getaway flights after a night game. But he knew the way home.

The Tigers began to win. They won a lot. Slightly dazed fans, who had forgotten what it was like, suddenly started poring over box scores in the daily papers, checking the standings, watching the scoreboard.

By mid-June the team already had won more games than in the entire 2003 season and, astonishingly, the Tigers had the best record in baseball.

"It isn't fair to Alan Trammell," Leyland said. "He didn't have the players in his seasons here that I have now."

To be more accurate, he had several of the players but they weren't playing like this. Ordoñez was not only healthy, he was enthused, hitting like he did when he was a star with the White Sox. Guillen, too, had recovered, and whatever had been bothering Pudge was forgotten. He was the player he used to be and assumed the position of head cheerleader on the bench.

But, as Leyland said, it was the supporting cast that made the difference. For the first time since coming to Comerica they had a center fielder in Curtis Granderson who could not only cover the vast reaches of the outfield but hit with power. Justin Verlander stepped out of his first year of professional ball and into the starting rotation. Joel Zumaya, who consistently threw in the 100-mile-an-hour range, became the set-up man out of the bullpen. A free-agent pickup that seemed puzzling at the time, 41-year-old left-hander Kenny Rogers, anchored the young pitching staff.

And an odd thing happened. Suddenly, Comerica Park wasn't such a bad place to be at all. It became the focus of a summer-long party, a celebration that spilled into the streets of its downtown neighborhood. Young fans who had never experienced a winning baseball team in Detroit discovered the joy of a pennant race.

Although the Tigers stumbled late in the season, they still made the playoffs as a wild card. But they were given little chance to survive the mighty Yankees in the first round.

After losing the first game, they took New York three in a row, including a Game 3 shutout by Rogers in an absolutely frenzied Comerica Park.

Rogers went on to pitch another shutout against Oakland in the league championship round, and the Tigers swept the A's, vaulting into the World Series on a ninth-inning three-run homer by Ordoñez. That celebration eclipsed everything that had gone before in this improbable year.

But the Tigers couldn't maintain the momentum in the Series after a one-week layoff. Repeated fielding mistakes, mostly on throwing errors by their pitchers, and a complete hitting collapse by the bulk of their starting lineup sent the team down to St. Louis in five games. Not before Rogers had pitched his third straight scoreless start, however, in one of the most remarkable performances in Detroit history.

Midway through the season, the city announced that old Tiger Stadium would finally be torn down. Although there was some grumbling, the predicted outcry never took place. Comerica Park had become the Tigers' true home at last. Winning made it a ballpark. Memories were being made.

# ANSWERS TO
# TRIVIA QUESTIONS

**Page 8:** Davy Jones was nicknamed Kangaroo because he jumped between the two major leagues so often.

**Page 12:** Cobb played before uniforms were numbered.

**Page 27:** The only man to pitch a perfect game against the Tigers was Charley Robertson, White Sox, April 30, 1922.

**Page 32:** Kirk Gibson left the broadcast booth in 2003 to become the Tigers top assistant coach.

**Page 47:** Frank Frisch was the other player-manager in the 1934 World Series.

**Page 54:** Paul Foytack and Jim Bunning, of the Tigers, and Jaime Navarro, of Milwaukee, are the only pitchers to give up two over-the-rooftop homers. Both of Foytack's were to Mickey Mantle.

**Page 58:** Earl Averill made his only trip to the World Series with the Tigers.

**Page 69:** Walt Dropo set a record by getting 12 straight hits after being traded to the Tigers.

**Page 73:** Three pitchers besides Virgil Trucks have thrown no-hitters for the Tigers. They were George Mullin, in 1912; Jim Bunning, in 1958; and Jack Morris, in 1984.

**Page 79:** Kaline replaced Don Lund. Kaline's last season as a full-time right fielder was 1971, and he was replaced by Jim Northrup.

**Page 98:** McLain failed to finish 13 of his 41 starts.

**Page 113:** Al Kaline and Eddie Mathews are the two Hall of Famers on that team.

**Page 127:** "Dancing in the Streets," by Martha Reeves and the Vandellas, was played at every home game during the 1984 season.

**Page 137:** Bill Gullickson, the Tigers' only 20-game winner of the 1990s, was 20–9 in 1991.

# Detroit Tigers All-Time Roster (through 2006 season)

This list includes anyone who ever played a game for the Tigers, including the college students who were recruited to take the field for one game in Philadelphia in 1912 when the regular players went on strike after Ty Cobb was suspended.

**A**

| | |
|---|---|
| Glenn Abbott (P) | 1983–84 |
| Al Aber (P) | 1953–57 |
| Juan Acevedo (P) | 2002 |
| Bob Adams (C) | 1977 |
| Hank Aguirre (P) | 1958–67 |
| Pat Ahearne (P) | 1995 |
| Eddie Ainsmith (C) | 1919–21 |
| Bill Akers (SS) | 1929–31 |
| Scott Aldred (P) | 1990–92, 1996 |
| Dale Alexander (1B) | 1929–32 |
| Doyle Alexander (P) | 1987–89 |
| Andy Allanson (C) | 1991 |
| Dusty Allen (2B) | 2000 |
| Rod Allen (OF) | 1984 |
| Ernie Alten (P) | 1920 |
| George Alusik (OF) | 1958, 1961–62 |
| Luis Alvarado (3B) | 1977 |
| Gabe Alvarez (3B) | 1998–2000 |
| Ossie Alvarez (SS) | 1959 |
| Sandy Amoros (OF) | 1960 |
| Bob Anderson (P) | 1963 |
| Matt Anderson (P) | 1998–2003 |
| Jimmy Archer (C) | 1907 |
| George Archie (1B) | 1938 |

| | |
|---|---|
| Harry Arndt (OF) | 1902 |
| Fernando Arroyo (P) | 1975, 1977–79 |
| Elden Auker (P) | 1933–38 |
| Brad Ausmus (C) | 1996, 1999–2000 |
| Earl Averill (OF) | 1939–40 |
| Steve Avery (P) | 2003 |
| Doc Ayers (P) | 1919–21 |

**B**

| | |
|---|---|
| Bill Bailey (P) | 1918 |
| Howard Bailey (P) | 1981–83 |
| Doug Bair (P) | 1983–85 |
| Del Baker (C) | 1914–16 |
| Doug Baker (SS) | 1984–87 |
| Steve Baker (P) | 1978–79 |
| Paul Bako (C) | 1998 |
| Billy Baldwin (OF) | 1975 |
| Chris Bando (C) | 1988 |
| Ray Bare (P) | 1975–77 |
| Clyde Barfoot (P) | 1926 |
| Frank Barnes (P) | 1929 |
| Sam Barnes (2B) | 1921 |
| Skeeter Barnes (3B) | 1991–94 |
| Jimmy Barrett (OF) | 1901–05 |
| Kimera Bartee (OF) | 1996–99 |
| Dick Bartell (SS) | 1940–41 |
| Al Bashang (OF) | 1912 |
| Johnny Bassler (C) | 1921–27 |
| Matt Batts (C) | 1952–54 |
| Paddy Baumann (2B) | 1911–14 |
| Harry Baumgartner (P) | 1920 |

| | | | |
|---|---|---|---|
| John Baumgartner (3B) | 1953 | Brian Bohanon (P) | 1995 |
| Danny Bautista (OF) | 1993–96 | Bernie Boland (P) | 1915–20 |
| Jose Bautista (P) | 1997 | Frank Bolling (2B) | 1954, 1956–60 |
| Trey Beamon (OF) | 1998 | Milt Bolling (SS) | 1958 |
| Billy Bean (OF) | 1987–89 | Cliff Bolton (C) | 1937 |
| Billy Beane (OF) | 1988 | Tom Bolton (P) | 1993 |
| Dave Beard (P) | 1989 | Jeremy Bonderman (P) | 2003–06 |
| Gene Bearden (P) | 1951 | Danny Boone (P) | 1921 |
| Erve Beck (1B) | 1902 | Ray Boone (3B) | 1953–58 |
| Walter Beck (P) | 1944 | Dave Borkowski (P) | 1999–2001 |
| Heinie Beckendorf (C) | 1909–10 | Red Borom (2B) | 1944–45 |
| Rich Becker (OF) | 2000 | Steve Boros (3B) | 1957–58, 1961–62 |
| Wayne Belardi (1B) | 1954–56 | Hank Borowy (P) | 1950–51 |
| Tim Belcher (P) | 1994 | Dave Boswell (P) | 1971 |
| Beau Bell (OF) | 1939 | Jim Brady (P) | 1956 |
| Al Benton (P) | 1938–42, 1945–48 | Ralph Branca (P) | 1953–54 |
| Lou Berberet (C) | 1959–60 | Jim Brideweser (2B) | 1956 |
| Juan Berenguer (P) | 1982–85 | Rocky Bridges (SS) | 1959–60 |
| Dave Bergman (1B) | 1984–92 | Tommy Bridges (P) | 1930–43, 1945–46 |
| Sean Bergman (P) | 1993–95 | Ed Brinkman (SS) | 1971–74 |
| Tony Bernazard (2B) | 1991 | Doug Brocail (P) | 1997–2000 |
| Adam Bernero (P) | 2000–03 | Rico Brogna (1B) | 1992 |
| Johnny Bero (2B) | 1948 | Ike Brookens (P) | 1975 |
| Geronimo Berroa (OF) | 1998 | Tom Brookens (3B) | 1979–88 |
| Neil Berry (2B) | 1948–52 | Lou Brower (SS) | 1931 |
| Reno Bertoia (3B) | 1953–58, 1961–62 | Chris Brown (3B) | 1989 |
| Jason Beverlin (P) | 2002 | Darrell Brown (OF) | 1981 |
| Monte Bevil (C) | 1904 | Dick Brown (C) | 1961–62 |
| Steve Bilko (1B) | 1960 | Gates Brown (OF) | 1963–75 |
| Jack Billingham (P) | 1978–80 | Ike Brown (2B) | 1969–74 |
| Josh Billings (P) | 1927–29 | Frank Browning (P) | 1910 |
| Babe Birrer (P) | 1955 | Bob Bruce (P) | 1959–61 |
| Bud Black (P) | 1952, 1955–56 | Andy Bruckmiller (P) | 1905 |
| Willie Blair (P) | 1997, 1999–2001 | Mike Brumley (SS) | 1989 |
| Ike Blessitt (OF) | 1972 | Arlo Brunsberg (C) | 1966 |
| Ben Blomdahl (P) | 1995 | Will Brunson (P) | 1998–99 |
| Jimmy Bloodworth (2B) | 1942–43, 1946 | Billy Bruton (OF) | 1961–64 |
| Lu Blue (1B) | 1921–27 | Johnny Bucha (C) | 1953 |
| Hiram Bocachica (OF) | 2002–03 | Don Buddin (SS) | 1962 |
| Doug Bochtler (P) | 1998 | Fritz Buelow (C) | 1901–04 |
| Randy Bockus (P) | 1989 | George Bullard (SS) | 1954 |
| George Boehler (P) | 1912–16 | Jim Bunning (P) | 1955–63 |
| Joe Boever (P) | 1993–95 | Les Burke (2B) | 1923–26 |
| John Bogart (P) | 1920 | Bill Burns (P) | 1912 |

| | | | |
|---|---|---|---|
| George Burns (1B) | 1914–17 | Dean Chance (P) | 1971 |
| Jack Burns (1B) | 1936 | Harry Chiti (C) | 1960–61 |
| Joe Burns (OF) | 1913 | Mike Chris (P) | 1979 |
| John Burns (2B) | 1903–04 | Neil Chrisley (OF) | 1959–60 |
| Pete Burnside (P) | 1959–60 | Bob Christian (1B) | 1968 |
| Sheldon Burnside (P) | 1978–79 | Mark Christman (3B) | 1938–39 |
| Donie Bush (SS) | 1908–21 | Mike Christopher (P) | 1995–96 |
| Sal Butera (C) | 1983 | Al Cicotte (P) | 1958 |
| Harry Byrd (P) | 1957 | Eddie Cicotte (P) | 1905 |
| | | Danny Claire (SS) | 1920 |
| **C** | | Danny Clark (2B) | 1922 |
| Enos Cabell (1B) | 1982–83 | Jermaine Clark (1B) | 2001 |
| Greg Cadaret (P) | 1994 | Mel Clark (OF) | 1957 |
| Bob Cain (P) | 1951 | Phil Clark (OF) | 1992 |
| Les Cain (P) | 1968, 1970–72 | Tony Clark (1B) | 1995–2001 |
| Paul Calvert (P) | 1950–51 | Nig Clarke (C) | 1905 |
| Bill Campbell (P) | 1986 | Rufe Clarke (P) | 1923–24 |
| Bruce Campbell (OF) | 1940–41 | Al Clauss (P) | 1913 |
| Dave Campbell (1B) | 1967–68 | Brent Clevlen (OF) | 2006 |
| Paul Campbell (1B) | 1948–50 | Flea Clifton (3B) | 1934–37 |
| Guy Cantrell (P) | 1930 | Joe Cobb (PH) | 1918 |
| George Cappuzzello (P) | 1981 | Ty Cobb (OF) | 1905–26 |
| Javier Cardona (C) | 2000–01 | Mickey Cochrane (C) | 1934–37 |
| Fred Carisch (C) | 1923 | Jack Coffey (2B) | 1918 |
| Charlie Carr (1B) | 1903–04 | Slick Coffman (P) | 1937–39 |
| Mark Carreon (OF) | 1992 | Rocky Colavito (OF) | 1960–63 |
| Ownie Carroll (P) | 1925, 1927–30 | Nate Colbert (1B) | 1975 |
| Frank Carswell (OF) | 1953 | Bert Cole (P) | 1921–25 |
| Chuck Cary (P) | 1985–86 | Joe Coleman Jr. (P) | 1971–76 |
| Jerry Casale (P) | 1961–62 | Joe Coleman Sr. (P) | 1955 |
| Raul Casanova (C) | 1996–98 | Vince Coleman (OF) | 1997 |
| Doc Casey (3B) | 1901–02 | Darnell Coles (3B) | 1986–87, 1990 |
| Joe Casey (C) | 1909–11 | Orlin Collier (P) | 1931 |
| Sean Casey (1B) | 2006 | Dave Collins (OF) | 1986 |
| Norm Cash (1B) | 1960–74 | Kevin Collins (3B) | 1970–71 |
| Ron Cash (1B) | 1973–74 | Rip Collins (P) | 1923–27 |
| George Caster (P) | 1945–46 | Roman Colon (P) | 2005–06 |
| Frank Castillo (P) | 1998 | Steve Colyer (P) | 2004 |
| Marty Castillo (3B) | 1981–85 | Wayne Comer (OF) | 1967–68, 1972 |
| Frank Catalanotto (2B) | 1997–99 | Ralph Comstock (P) | 1913 |
| Pug Cavet (P) | 1911, 1914–15 | Dick Conger (P) | 1940 |
| Andujar Cedeño (SS) | 1996 | Allen Conkwright (P) | 1920 |
| Roger Cedeño (OF) | 2001 | Bill Connelly (P) | 1950 |
| John Cerutti (P) | 1991 | Earl Cook (P) | 1941 |

| | | | |
|---|---|---|---|
| Dick Cooley (OF) | 1905 | Doc Daugherty (PH) | 1951 |
| Jack Coombs (P) | 1920 | Hooks Dauss (P) | 1912–26 |
| Wilbur Cooper (P) | 1926 | Jerry Davie (P) | 1959 |
| Tim Corcoran (OF) | 1977–80 | Eric Davis (OF) | 1993–94 |
| Francisco Cordero (P) | 1999 | Harry Davis (1B) | 1932–33 |
| Nate Cornejo (P) | 2001–04 | Storm Davis (P) | 1993–94 |
| Chuck Cottier (2B) | 1961 | Woody Davis (P) | 1938 |
| Johnny Couch (P) | 1917 | Charlie Deal (3B) | 1912–13 |
| Bill Coughlin (3B) | 1904–08 | Rob Deer (OF) | 1991–93 |
| Ernie Courtney (3B) | 1903 | John Deering (P) | 1903 |
| Harry Coveleski (P) | 1914–18 | Tony DeFate (2B) | 1917 |
| Bill Covington (P) | 1911–12 | Ivan DeJesus (SS) | 1988 |
| Al Cowens (OF) | 1980–81 | Mark DeJohn (SS) | 1982 |
| Red Cox (P) | 1920 | Jim Delahanty (2B) | 1909–12 |
| Doc Cramer (OF) | 1942–48 | Luis de los Santos (OF) | 1991 |
| Jim Crawford (P) | 1976–78 | Jim Delsing (OF) | 1952–56 |
| Sam Crawford (OF) | 1903–17 | Don Demeter (OF) | 1964–66 |
| Doug Creek (P) | 2005 | Steve Demeter (3B) | 1959 |
| Jack Crimian (P) | 1957 | Ray Demmitt (OF) | 1914 |
| Leo Cristante (P) | 1955 | Bill Denehy (P) | 1971 |
| Davey Crockett (1B) | 1901 | Gene Desautels (C) | 1930–33 |
| Jack Cronin (P) | 1901–02 | John DeSilva (P) | 1993 |
| Frank Croucher (SS) | 1939–41 | Bernie DeViveiros (SS) | 1927 |
| Dean Crow (P) | 1998 | Bob Didier (C) | 1973 |
| Alvin Crowder (P) | 1934–36 | Mike DiFelice (C) | 2004 |
| Ray Crumpler (P) | 1920 | Steve Dillard (2B) | 1978 |
| Deivi Cruz (2B) | 1997–2001 | Pop Dillon (1B) | 1901–02 |
| Fausto Cruz (2B) | 1996 | Craig Dingman (P) | 2004–05 |
| Jacob Cruz (OF) | 2002 | George Disch (P) | 1905 |
| Nelson Cruz (P) | 1999–2000 | Glenn Dishman (P) | 1997 |
| Roy Cullenbine (OF) | 1938–39, 1945–47 | Jack Dittmer (3B) | 1957 |
| John Cummings (P) | 1996–97 | Pat Dobson (P) | 1967–69 |
| George Cunningham (P) | 1916–19, 1921 | Larry Doby (OF) | 1959 |
| Jim Curry (2B) | 1918 | John Doherty (P) | 1992–95 |
| Chad Curtis (OF) | 1995–96 | Frank Doljack (OF) | 1930–34 |
| George Cutshaw (2B) | 1922–23 | Red Donahue (P) | 1906 |
| Milt Cuyler (OF) | 1990–95 | Jim Donohue (P) | 1961 |
| | | Bill Donovan (P) | 1903–12, 1918 |
| **D** | | Dick Donovan (P) | 1954 |
| Jack Dalton (OF) | 1916 | Tim Doran (C) | 1905 |
| Mike Dalton (P) | 1991 | Sean Douglass (P) | 2005 |
| Chuck Daniel (P) | 1957 | Snooks Dowd (P)inch runner | 1919 |
| Vic Darensbourg (P) | 2005 | Red Downs (2B) | 1907–08 |
| Jeff Datz (C) | 1989 | Jess Doyle (P) | 1925–27 |

| | |
|---|---|
| Delos Drake (OF) | 1911 |
| Lee Dressen (1B) | 1918 |
| Lew Drill (C) | 1904–05 |
| Walt Dropo (1B) | 1952–54 |
| Brian DuBois (P) | 1989–90 |
| Jean Dubuc (P) | 1912–16 |
| Joe Dugan (3B) | 1931 |
| Roberto Duran (P) | 1997–98 |
| Chad Durbin (P) | 2006 |
| Bob Dustal (P) | 1963 |
| Ben Dyer (3B) | 1916–19 |
| Duffy Dyer (C) | 1980–81 |

**E**

| | |
|---|---|
| Scott Earl (2B) | 1984 |
| Damion Easley (2B) | 1996–2002 |
| Mal Eason (P) | 1903 |
| Paul Easterling (OF) | 1928, 1930 |
| Zeb Eaton (P) | 1944–45 |
| Eric Eckenstahler (P) | 2002–03 |
| Dick Egan (P) | 1963–64 |
| Wish Egan (P) | 1902 |
| Howard Ehmke (P) | 1916–17, 1919–22 |
| Joey Eischen (P) | 1996 |
| Harry Eisenstat (P) | 1938–39 |
| Kid Elberfeld (SS) | 1901–03 |
| Heinie Elder (P) | 1913 |
| Babe Ellison (1B) | 1916–20 |
| Juan Encarnacion (OF) | 1997–2001 |
| Dave Engle (1B) | 1986 |
| Gil English (2B) | 1936–37 |
| John Ennis (P) | 2004 |
| Eric Erickson (P) | 1916, 1918–19 |
| Hal Erickson (P) | 1953 |
| Tex Erwin (C) | 1907 |
| John Eubank (P) | 1905–07 |
| Darrell Evans (1B) | 1984–88 |
| Hoot Evers (OF) | 1942, 1946–52, 1954 |

**F**

| | |
|---|---|
| Roy Face (P) | 1968 |
| Bill Fahey (C) | 1981–83 |
| Ferris Fain (1B) | 1955 |
| Bob Farley (OF) | 1962 |

| | |
|---|---|
| Ed Farmer (P) | 1973 |
| Jeff Farnsworth (P) | 2002 |
| Kyle Farnsworth (P) | 2005 |
| John Farrell (P) | 1996 |
| Bill Faul (P) | 1962–64 |
| Al Federoff (2B) | 1951–52 |
| Junior Felix (OF) | 1994 |
| Jack Feller (C) | 1958 |
| Chico Fernandez (SS) | 1960–63 |
| Cy Ferry (P) | 1904 |
| Robert Fick (C) | 1998–2002 |
| Mark Fidrych (P) | 1976–80 |
| Cecil Fielder (1B) | 1990–96 |
| Bruce Fields (OF) | 1986 |
| Jim Finigan (3B) | 1957 |
| Happy Finneran (P) | 1918 |
| Bill Fischer (P) | 1958, 1960–61 |
| Carl Fischer (P) | 1933–35 |
| Ed Fisher (P) | 1902 |
| Fritz Fisher (P) | 1964 |
| Ira Flagstead (OF) | 1917, 1919–23 |
| John Flaherty (C) | 1994–96 |
| Les Fleming (OF) | 1939 |
| Scott Fletcher (2B) | 1995 |
| Tom Fletcher (P) | 1962 |
| Van Fletcher (P) | 1955 |
| Bryce Florie (P) | 1998–99 |
| Ben Flowers (P) | 1955 |
| Bubba Floyd (SS) | 1944 |
| Doug Flynn (2B) | 1985 |
| Hank Foiles (C) | 1960 |
| Jim Foor (P) | 1971–72 |
| Gene Ford (P) | 1905 |
| Larry Foster (P) | 1963 |
| Bob Fothergill (OF) | 1922–30 |
| Steve Foucault (P) | 1977–78 |
| Terry Fox (P) | 1961–66 |
| Paul Foytack (P) | 1953, 1955–63 |
| Ray Francis (P) | 1923 |
| Tito Francona (OF) | 1958 |
| Murray Franklin (SS) | 1941–42 |
| Vic Frasier (P) | 1933–34 |
| Bill Freehan (C) | 1961, 1963–76 |
| George Freese (PH) | 1953 |

| | | | | |
|---|---|---|---|---|
| Cy Fried (P) | 1920 | Fred Gladding (P) | 1961–67 |
| Own Friend (2B) | 1953 | John Glaiser (P) | 1920 |
| Emil Frisk (P) | 1901 | Kid Gleason (2B) | 1901–02 |
| Bill Froats (P) | 1955 | Jerry Don Gleaton (P) | 1990–91 |
| Travis Fryman (3B) | 1990–97 | Ed Glynn (P) | 1975–78 |
| Woody Fryman (P) | 1972–74 | Greg Gohr (P) | 1993–96 |
| Charlie Fuchs (P) | 1942 | Izzy Goldstein (P) | 1932 |
| Tito Fuentes (2B) | 1977 | Purnal Goldy (OF) | 1962–63 |
| Frank Fuller (2B) | 1915–16 | Alexis Gomez (OF) | 2005–06 |
| Liz Funk (OF) | 1930 | Chris Gomez (SS) | 1993–96 |
| | | Dan Gonzales (OF) | 1979–80 |
| **G** | | Juan Gonzalez (OF) | 2000 |
| Chick Gagnon (SS) | 1922 | Julio Gonzalez (SS) | 1983 |
| Eddie Gailliard (P) | 1997 | Luis Gonzalez (OF) | 1998 |
| Del Gainor (1B) | 1909, 1911–14 | Andrew Good (P) | 2005 |
| Dan Gakeler (P) | 1991 | Johnny Gorsica (P) | 1940–44, 1946–47 |
| Doug Gallagher (P) | 1962 | Goose Goslin (OF) | 1934–37 |
| Chick Galloway (SS) | 1928 | John Grabowski (C) | 1931 |
| John Gamble (SS) | 1972–73 | Bill Graham (P) | 1966 |
| Barbaro Garbey (1B) | 1984–85 | Kyle Graham (P) | 1929 |
| Alex Garbowski (P)inch runner | 1952 | Curtis Granderson (OF) | 2004–06 |
| Karim Garcia (OF) | 1999–2000 | Mark Grater (P) | 1993 |
| Luis Garcia (SS) | 1999 | Beiker Graterol (P) | 1999 |
| Pedro Garcia (2B) | 1976 | Ted Gray (P) | 1946, 1948–54 |
| Mike Gardiner (P) | 1993–95 | Lenny Green (OF) | 1967–68 |
| Ned Garver (P) | 1952–56 | Hank Greenberg (1B) | 1930, 1933–41, 1945–46 |
| Charlie Gehringer (2B) | 1924–42 | Altar Greene (OF) | 1979 |
| Charley Gelbert (SS) | 1937 | Paddy Greene (3B) | 1903 |
| Rufe Gentry (P) | 1943–44, 1946–48 | Seth Greisinger (P) | 1998, 2002 |
| Franklyn German (P) | 2002–05 | Ed Gremminger (3B) | 1904 |
| Dick Gernert (1B) | 1960–61 | Art Griggs (1B) | 1918 |
| Doc Gessler (OF) | 1903 | Jason Grilli (P) | 2005–06 |
| Tony Giarratano (SS) | 2005 | Steve Grilli (P) | 1975–77 |
| Frank Gibson (C) | 1913 | Marv Grissom (P) | 1949 |
| Kirk Gibson (OF) | 1979–87, 1993–95 | Steve Gromek (P) | 1953–57 |
| Paul Gibson (P) | 1988–91 | Buddy Groom (P) | 1992–95 |
| Sam Gibson (P) | 1926–28 | Johnny Groth (OF) | 1946–52, 1957–60 |
| Floyd Giebell (P) | 1939–41 | Bert Grover (P) | 1913 |
| Bill Gilbreth (P) | 1971–72 | John Grubb (OF) | 1983–87 |
| George Gill (P) | 1937–39 | Joe Grzenda (P) | 1961 |
| Bob Gillespie (P) | 1944 | Carlos Guillen (SS) | 2004–06 |
| Joe Ginsberg (C) | 1948, 1950–53 | Bill Gullickson (P) | 1991–94 |
| Matt Ginter (P) | 2005 | Dave Gumpert (P) | 1982–83 |
| Dan Gladden (OF) | 1992–93 | Cesar Gutierrez (SS) | 1969–71 |

**H**

| | |
|---|---|
| David Haas (P) | 1991–93 |
| Sammy Hale (3B) | 1920–21 |
| Charley Hall (P) | 1918 |
| Herb Hall (P) | 1918 |
| Joe Hall (OF) | 1995, 1997 |
| Marc Hall (P) | 1913–14 |
| Tom Haller (C) | 1972 |
| Shane Halter (SS) | 2000–03 |
| Bob Hamelin (DH) | 1997 |
| Earl Hamilton (P) | 1916 |
| Jack Hamilton (P) | 1964–65 |
| Luke Hamlin (P) | 1933–34 |
| Fred Haney (3B) | 1922–25 |
| Don Hankins (P) | 1927 |
| Jack Hannahan (1B) | 2006 |
| Jim Hannan (P) | 1971 |
| Charlie Harding (P) | 1913 |
| Shawn Hare (OF) | 1991–92 |
| Pinky Hargrave (C) | 1928–30 |
| Dick Harley (OF) | 1902 |
| Brian Harper (OF) | 1986 |
| George Harper (OF) | 1916–18 |
| Terry Harper (OF) | 1987 |
| Denny Harriger (P) | 1998 |
| Andy Harrington (PH) | 1925 |
| Bob Harris (P) | 1938–39 |
| Bucky Harris (2B) | 1929, 1931 |
| Gail Harris (1B) | 1958–60 |
| Gene Harris (P) | 1994 |
| Ned Harris (OF) | 1941–43, 1946 |
| Earl Harrist (P) | 1953 |
| Bill Haselman (C) | 1999 |
| Fred Hatfield (2B) | 1952–56 |
| Clyde Hatter (P) | 1935, 1937 |
| Brad Havens (P) | 1989 |
| Ray Hayworth (C) | 1926, 1929–38 |
| Bob Hazel (OF) | 1958 |
| Bill Heath (C) | 1967 |
| Mike Heath (C) | 1986–90 |
| Richie Hebner (1B) | 1980–82 |
| Don Heffner (2B) | 1944 |
| Jim Hegan (C) | 1958 |
| Harry Heilmann (OF) | 1914, 1916–29 |

| | |
|---|---|
| Don Heinkel (P) | 1988 |
| Mike Henneman (P) | 1987–95 |
| Les Hennessy (2B) | 1913 |
| Oscar Henriquez (P) | 2002 |
| Dwayne Henry (P) | 1995 |
| Roy Henshaw (P) | 1942–44 |
| Ray Herbert (P) | 1950–51, 1953–54 |
| Babe Herman (OF) | 1937 |
| Fernando Hernandez (P) | 1997 |
| Willie Hernandez (P) | 1984–89 |
| Larry Herndon (OF) | 1982–88 |
| Art Herring (P) | 1929–33 |
| Whitey Herzog (OF) | 1963 |
| Gus Hetling (3B) | 1906 |
| Phil Hiatt (3B) | 1996 |
| Piano Legs Hickman (OF) | 1904–05 |
| Buddy Hicks (SS) | 1956 |
| Pinky Higgins (3B) | 1939–44, 1946 |
| Bobby Higginson (OF) | 1995–2005 |
| Ed High (P) | 1901 |
| Hugo High (OF) | 1913–14 |
| Erik Hiljus (P) | 1999–2000 |
| John Hiller (P) | 1965–70, 1972–80 |
| A.J. Hinch (C) | 2003 |
| Billy Hitchcock (SS) | 1942, 1946, 1953 |
| Billy Hoeft (P) | 1952–59 |
| Elon Hogsett (P) | 1929–36, 1944 |
| Fred Holdsworth (P) | 1972–74 |
| Carl Holling (P) | 1921–22 |
| Ken Holloway (P) | 1922–28 |
| Shawn Holman (P) | 1989 |
| Ducky Holmes (OF) | 1901–02 |
| Chris Holt (P) | 2001 |
| Vern Holtgrave (P) | 1965 |
| Kevin Hooper (2B) | 2005–06 |
| Joe Hoover (SS) | 1943–45 |
| John Hopp (1B) | 1952 |
| Willie Horton (OF) | 1963–77 |
| Tim Hosley (C) | 1970–71 |
| Gene Host (P) | 1956 |
| Chuck Hostetler (OF) | 1944–45 |
| Frank House (C) | 1950–51, 1954–57, 1961 |
| Will House (P) | 1913 |
| Art Houtteman (P) | 1945–50, 1952–53 |

| | |
|---|---|
| Frank Howard (1B) | 1972–73 |
| Waite Hoyt (P) | 1930–31 |
| Clarence Huber (3B) | 1920–21 |
| Charles Hudson (P) | 1989 |
| Frank Huelsman (OF) | 1904 |
| Tom Hughes (OF) | 1930 |
| Mark Huismann (P) | 1988 |
| Terry Humphrey (C) | 1975 |
| Bob Humphreys (P) | 1962 |
| Brian Hunter (OF) | 1997–99 |
| Jimmy Hurst (OF) | 1997 |
| Fred Hutchinson (P) | 1939–41, 1946–53 |
| Tim Hyers (1B) | 1996 |

## I

| | |
|---|---|
| Gary Ignasiak (P) | 1973 |
| Pete Incaviglia (OF) | 1991, 1998 |
| Omar Infante (2B) | 2002–06 |
| Brandon Inge (3B) | 2001–06 |
| Riccardo Ingram (OF) | 1994 |
| Ed Irvin (3B) | 1912 |
| Mike Ivie (DH) | 1982–83 |

## J

| | |
|---|---|
| Charlie Jackson (P) | 1905 |
| Damian Jackson (SS) | 2002 |
| Ron Jackson (1B) | 1981 |
| Ryan Jackson (OF) | 2001–02 |
| Baby Doll Jacobson (OF) | 1915 |
| Charlie Jaeger (P) | 1904 |
| Art James (OF) | 1975 |
| Bill James (P) | 1915–19 |
| Bob James (P) | 1982–83 |
| Kevin Jarvis (P) | 1997 |
| Paul Jata (1B) | 1972 |
| Gregg Jefferies (DH) | 1999–2000 |
| Hughie Jennings (PH) | 1907, 1909, 1912, 1918 |
| Bill Jensen (P) | 1912 |
| Marcus Jensen (C) | 1997 |
| Jason Jimenez (P) | 2002 |
| Augie Johns (P) | 1926–27 |
| Alex Johnson (OF) | 1976 |
| Brian Johnson (C) | 1997 |
| Dave Johnson (P) | 1993 |

| | |
|---|---|
| Earl Johnson (P) | 1951 |
| Howard Johnson (3B) | 1982–84 |
| Jason Johnson (P) | 2004–05 |
| Ken Johnson (P) | 1952 |
| Mark Johnson (P) | 2000 |
| Roy Johnson (OF) | 1929–32 |
| Sylvester Johnson (P) | 1922–25 |
| Alex Jones (P) | 1903 |
| Bob Jones (3B) | 1917–25 |
| Dalton Jones (2B) | 1970–72 |
| Davy Jones (OF) | 1906–12 |
| Deacon Jones (P) | 1916–18 |
| Elijah Jones (P) | 1907, 1909 |
| Ken Jones (P) | 1924 |
| Lynn Jones (OF) | 1979–83 |
| Ruppert Jones (OF) | 1984 |
| Sam Jones (P) | 1962 |
| Todd Jones (P) | 1997–2001, 2006 |
| Tom Jones (1B) | 1909–10 |
| Tracy Jones (OF) | 1989–90 |
| Milt Jordan (P) | 1953 |
| Walt Justis (P) | 1905 |

## K

| | |
|---|---|
| Jeff Kaiser (P) | 1991 |
| Al Kaline (OF) | 1953–74 |
| Rudy Kallio (P) | 1918–19 |
| Harry Kane (P) | 1903 |
| Gabe Kapler (OF) | 1998–99 |
| Jason Karnuth (P) | 2005 |
| Marty Kavanagh (2B) | 1914–16 |
| Greg Keagle (P) | 1996–98 |
| George Kell (3B) | 1946–52 |
| Mick Kelleher (3B) | 1981 |
| Charlie Keller (OF) | 1950–51 |
| Kris Keller (P) | 2002 |
| Bryan Kelly (P) | 1986–87 |
| Steve Kemp (OF) | 1977–81 |
| Bob Kennedy (OF) | 1956 |
| Vern Kennedy (P) | 1938–39 |
| Russ Kerns (PH) | 1945 |
| John Kerr (SS) | 1923–24 |
| Masao Kida (P) | 1999–2000 |
| John Kiely (P) | 1991–93 |

| | | | | |
|---|---|---|---|---|
| Mike Kilkenny (P) | 1969–72 | Lerrin LaGrow (P) | 1970, 1972–75 |
| Red Killefer (2B) | 1907–09 | Eddie Lake (SS) | 1946–50 |
| Ed Killian (P) | 1904–10 | Joe Lake (P) | 1912–13 |
| Bruce Kimm (C) | 1976–77 | Al Lakeman (C) | 1954 |
| Chad Kimsey (P) | 1936 | Gene Lamont (C) | 1970–72, 1974–75 |
| Chick King (OF) | 1954–56 | Les Lancaster (P) | 1992 |
| Eric King (P) | 1986–88, 1992 | Jim Landis (OF) | 1967 |
| Gene Kingsale (OF) | 2002 | Marvin Lane (OF) | 1971–74, 1976 |
| Dennis Kinney (P) | 1981 | Dave LaPoint (P) | 1986 |
| Matt Kinzer (P) | 1990 | Steve Larkin (P) | 1934 |
| Jay Kirke (2B) | 1910 | Frank Lary (P) | 1954–64 |
| Rube Kisinger (P) | 1902–03 | Fred Lasher (P) | 1967–70 |
| Frank Kitson (P) | 1903–05 | Chuck Lathers (3B) | 1910–11 |
| Danny Klassen (3B) | 2003 | Charlie Lau (C) | 1956, 1958–59 |
| Al Klawitter (P) | 1913 | Bill Lawrence (OF) | 1932 |
| Ron Kline (P) | 1961–62 | Roxie Lawson (P) | 1933, 1935–39 |
| Johnny Klippstein (P) | 1967 | Bill Laxton (P) | 1976 |
| Rudy Kneisch (P) | 1926 | Jack Lazorko (P) | 1986 |
| Ray Knight (1B) | 1988 | Rick Leach (1B) | 1981–83 |
| Gary Knotts (P) | 2003–04 | Razor Ledbetter (P) | 1915 |
| John Knox (2B) | 1972–75 | Wil Ledezma (P) | 2003–06 |
| Kurt Knudsen (P) | 1992–94 | Don Lee (P) | 1957–58 |
| Al Koch (P) | 1963–64 | Ron LeFlore (OF) | 1974–79 |
| Brad Kocher (C) | 1912 | Bill Leinhauser (OF) | 1912 |
| Mark Koenig (SS) | 1930–31 | Mark Leiter (P) | 1991–93 |
| Don Kolloway (1B) | 1949–52 | Bill Lelivelt (P) | 1909–10 |
| Howie Koplitz (P) | 1961–62 | Dave Lemanczyk (P) | 1973–76 |
| George Korince (P) | 1966–67 | Chet Lemon (OF) | 1982–90 |
| Frank Kostro (3B) | 1962–63 | Don Lenhardt (OF) | 1952 |
| Wayne Krenchicki (3B) | 1983 | Jim Lentine (OF) | 1980 |
| Chuck Kress (1B) | 1954 | Dutch Leonard (P) | 1919–21, 1924–25 |
| Red Kress (3B) | 1939–40 | Ted Lepcio (SS) | 1959 |
| Lou Kretlow (P) | 1946, 1948–49 | Peter LePine (OF) | 1902 |
| Chad Kreuter (C) | 1992–94 | George Lerchen (OF) | 1952 |
| Bill Krueger (P) | 1993–94 | Don Leshnock (P) | 1972 |
| Dick Kryhoski (1B) | 1950–51 | Al Levine (P) | 2004 |
| Harvey Kuenn (SS) | 1952–59 | Colby Lewis (P) | 2006 |
| Rusty Kuntz (OF) | 1984–85 | Mark Lewis (2B) | 1996 |
| | | Richie Lewis (P) | 1996 |
| **L** | | José Lima (P) | 1994–96, 2001–02 |
| Chet Laabs (OF) | 1937–39 | Em Lindbeck (PH) | 1960 |
| Clem Labine (P) | 1960 | Jim Lindeman (1B) | 1990 |
| Ed Lafitte (P) | 1909, 1911–12 | Chris Lindsay (1B) | 1905–06 |
| Mike Laga (1B) | 1982–86 | Rod Lindsey (OF) | 2000 |

| | |
|---|---|
| Carl Linhart (PH) | 1952 |
| Johnny Lipon (SS) | 1942, 1946, 1948–52 |
| Felipe Lira (P) | 1995–97, 1999 |
| Dick Littlefield (P) | 1952 |
| Jack Lively (P) | 1911 |
| Scott Livingstone (3B) | 1991–94 |
| Harry Lochhead (SS) | 1901 |
| Bob Logan (P) | 1937 |
| Nook Logan (OF) | 2004–05 |
| Mickey Lolich (P) | 1963–75 |
| George Lombard (OF) | 2002 |
| Herman Long (SS) | 1903 |
| Aurelio Lopez (P) | 1979–85 |
| Lefty Lorenzen (P) | 1913 |
| Art Loudell (P) | 1910 |
| Baldy Louden (2B) | 1912–13 |
| Shane Loux (P) | 2002–03 |
| Slim Love (P) | 1919–20 |
| Torey Lovullo (1B) | 1988–89 |
| Grover Lowdermilk (P) | 1915–16 |
| Bobby Lowe (2B) | 1904–07 |
| Dwight Lowry (C) | 1984, 1986–87 |
| Willie Ludolph (P) | 1924 |
| Urbano Lugo (P) | 1990 |
| Jerry Lumpe (2B) | 1964–67 |
| Don Lund (OF) | 1949, 1952–54 |
| Scott Lusader (OF) | 1987–90 |
| Billy Lush (OF) | 1903 |
| Fred Lynn (OF) | 1988–89 |
| Red Lynn (P) | 1939 |

**M**

| | |
|---|---|
| Duke Maas (P) | 1955–57 |
| Frank MacCormack (P) | 1976 |
| Bob MacDonald (P) | 1993 |
| Dave Machemer (2B) | 1979 |
| Jose Macias (2B) | 1999–2002 |
| Morris Madden (P) | 1987 |
| Elliott Maddox (OF) | 1970 |
| Dave Madison (P) | 1952–53 |
| Scotti Madison (3B) | 1985–86 |
| Bill Madlock (1B) | 1987 |
| Wendell Magee Jr. (OF) | 2000–02 |
| Billy Maharg (3B) | 1912 |

| | |
|---|---|
| Mickey Mahler (P) | 1985 |
| Bob Maier (3B) | 1945 |
| Alex Main (P) | 1914 |
| Tom Makowski (P) | 1975 |
| Herm Malloy (P) | 1907–08 |
| Harry Malmberg (2B) | 1955 |
| Hal Manders (P) | 1941–42, 1946 |
| Clyde Manion (C) | 1920–24, 1926–27 |
| Phil Mankowski (3B) | 1976–79 |
| Jeff Manto (1B) | 1998 |
| Jerry Manuel (2B) | 1975–76 |
| Heinie Manush (OF) | 1923–27 |
| Cliff Mapes (OF) | 1952 |
| Firpo Marberry (P) | 1933–35 |
| Leo Marentette (P) | 1965 |
| Dick Marlowe (P) | 1951–56 |
| Mike Maroth (P) | 2002–06 |
| Buck Marrow (P) | 1932 |
| Mike Marshall (P) | 1967 |
| Billy Martin (SS) | 1958 |
| John Martin (P) | 1983 |
| Ramon Martinez (3B) | 2005 |
| Roger Mason (P) | 1984 |
| Walt Masterson (P) | 1956 |
| Tom Matchick (SS) | 1967–69 |
| Eddie Mathews (1B) | 1967–68 |
| Bob Mavis (PR) | 1949 |
| Brian Maxcy (P) | 1995–96 |
| Charlie Maxwell (OF) | 1955–62 |
| Milt May (C) | 1976–79 |
| Eddie Mayo (2B) | 1944–48 |
| Sport McAllister (OF) | 1901–03 |
| Dick McAuliffe (2B) | 1960–73 |
| Arch McCarthy (P) | 1902 |
| Barney McCosky (OF) | 1939–42, 1946 |
| Benny McCoy (2B) | 1938–39 |
| Ed McCreery (P) | 1914 |
| Lance McCullers (P) | 1990 |
| Jeff McCurry (P) | 1996 |
| Mickey McDermott (P) | 1958 |
| Red McDermott (OF) | 1912 |
| Allen McDill (P) | 2000 |
| John McDonald (SS) | 2005 |
| Orlando McFarlane (C) | 1966 |

| | | | |
|---|---|---|---|
| Jim McGarr (2B) | 1912 | Orlando Miller (SS) | 1997 |
| Dan McGarvey (OF) | 1912 | Roscoe Miller (P) | 1901–02 |
| Pat McGehee (P) | 1912 | Trever Miller (P) | 1996 |
| Deacon McGuire (C) | 1902–03, 1912 | Zack Miner (P) | 2006 |
| John McHale (1B) | 1943–45, 1947–48 | Clarence Mitchell (P) | 1911 |
| Matty McIntyre (OF) | 1904–10 | Willie Mitchell (P) | 1916–19 |
| Archie McKain (P) | 1939–41 | Dave Mlicki (P) | 1999–2001 |
| Red McKee (C) | 1913–16 | Brian Moehler (P) | 1996–2002 |
| Denny McLain (P) | 1963–70 | Herb Moford (P) | 1958 |
| Pat McLaughlin (P) | 1937, 1945 | Bobby Molinaro (OF) | 1975, 1977, 1983 |
| Wayne McLeland (P) | 1951–52 | Bill Monbouquette (P) | 1966–67 |
| Sam McMackin (P) | 1902 | Sid Monge (P) | 1984 |
| Don McMahon (P) | 1968–69 | Craig Monroe (OF) | 2002–06 |
| Frank McManus (C) | 1904 | Manny Montejo (P) | 1961 |
| Marty McManus (3B) | 1927–31 | Anse Moore (OF) | 1946 |
| Billy McMillon (OF) | 2000–01 | Bill Moore (P) | 1925 |
| Fred McMullin (SS) | 1914 | Jackie Moore (C) | 1965 |
| Carl McNabb (PH) | 1945 | Mike Moore (P) | 1993–95 |
| Eric McNair (SS) | 1941–42 | Roy Moore (P) | 1922–23 |
| Norm McRae (P) | 1969–70 | Jake Mooty (P) | 1944 |
| Bill McTigue (P) | 1916 | Jerry Morales (OF) | 1979 |
| Rusty Meacham (P) | 1991 | Harry Moran (P) | 1912 |
| Pat Meany (SS) | 1912 | Keith Moreland (1B) | 1989 |
| Chris Mears (P) | 2003 | Chet Morgan (OF) | 1935, 1938 |
| Phil Meeler (P) | 1972 | Tom Morgan (P) | 1958–60 |
| Mitch Meluskey (C) | 2001–02 | George Moriarty (3B) | 1909–15 |
| Bob Melvin (C) | 1985 | Hal Morris (1B) | 2000 |
| Orlando Mercado (C) | 1987 | Jack Morris (P) | 1977–90 |
| Win Mercer (P) | 1902 | Warren Morris (2B) | 2003 |
| Herm Merritt (SS) | 1921 | Bill Morrisette (P) | 1920 |
| Scat Metha (2B) | 1940 | Jim Morrison (3B) | 1987–88 |
| Charlie Metro (OF) | 1943–44 | Bubba Morton (OF) | 1961–63 |
| Dan Meyer (OF) | 1974–76 | Lloyd Moseby (OF) | 1990–91 |
| Dutch Meyer (2B) | 1940–42 | Gerry Moses (C) | 1974 |
| Dan Miceli (P) | 1997 | John Moses (OF) | 1991 |
| Gene Michael (SS) | 1975 | Don Mossi (P) | 1959–63 |
| Jim Middleton (P) | 1921 | Les Mueller (P) | 1941, 1945 |
| Ed Mierkowicz (OF) | 1945, 1947–48 | Billy Mullen (3B) | 1926 |
| Andrew Miller (P) | 2006 | George Mullin (P) | 1902–13 |
| Bob G. Miller (P) | 1953–56 | Pat Mullin (OF) | 1941–42, 1946–53 |
| Bob L. Miller (P) | 1973 | Mike Munoz (P) | 1991–93 |
| Ed Miller (OF) | 1982 | Eric Munson (3B) | 2000–04 |
| Hack Miller (C) | 1944–45 | Dwayne Murphy (OF) | 1988 |
| Matt Miller (P) | 2001–02 | John Murphy (SS) | 1903 |

| | |
|---|---|
| Heath Murray (P) | 2001 |
| Glenn Myatt (C) | 1936 |
| Mike Myers (P) | 1995–97 |

## N

| | |
|---|---|
| Russ Nagelson (OF) | 1970 |
| Bill Nahorodny (PH) | 1983 |
| Doc Nance (OF) | 1901 |
| Ray Narleski (P) | 1959 |
| Julio Navarro (P) | 1964–66 |
| Bots Nekola (P) | 1933 |
| Lynn Nelson (P) | 1940 |
| Jack Ness (1B) | 1911 |
| Jim Nettles (OF) | 1974 |
| Johnny Neun (1B) | 1925–28 |
| Phil Nevin (OF) | 1995–97 |
| Hal Newhouser (P) | 1939–53 |
| Bobo Newsom (P) | 1939–41 |
| Simon Nicholls (SS) | 1903 |
| Fred Nicholson (OF) | 1917 |
| Joe Niekro (P) | 1970–72 |
| Bob Nieman (OF) | 1953–54 |
| Melvin Nieves (OF) | 1996–97 |
| Ron Nischwitz (P) | 1961–62, 1965 |
| C.J. Nitkowski (P) | 1995–96, 1999–2001 |
| Matt Nokes (C) | 1986–90 |
| Dickie Noles (P) | 1987 |
| Hideo Nomo (P) | 2000 |
| Lou North (P) | 1913 |
| Jim Northrup (OF) | 1964–74 |
| Greg Norton (1B) | 2004 |
| Randy Nosek (P) | 1989–90 |
| Roberto Novoa (P) | 2004 |
| Edwin Nunez (P) | 1989–90 |

## O

| | |
|---|---|
| Prince Oana (P) | 1943, 1945 |
| John O'Connell (2B) | 1902 |
| Ben Oglivie (OF) | 1974–77 |
| Frank Okrie (P) | 1920 |
| Red Oldham (P) | 1914–15, 1920–22 |
| Charley O'Leary (SS) | 1904–12 |
| Omar Olivares (P) | 1996–97 |
| Joe Oliver (C) | 1998 |

| | |
|---|---|
| Ole Olsen (P) | 1922–23 |
| Gregg Olson (P) | 1996 |
| Karl Olson (OF) | 1957 |
| Ollie O'Mara (SS) | 1912 |
| Randy O'Neal (P) | 1984–86 |
| Eddie Onslow (1B) | 1912–13 |
| Jack Onslow (C) | 1912 |
| Magglio Ordoñez (OF) | 2005–06 |
| Joe Orengo (SS) | 1944 |
| Frank O'Rourke (2B) | 1924–26 |
| Joe Orrell (P) | 1943–45 |
| Bobo Osborne (1B) | 1957–59, 1961–62 |
| Jimmy Outlaw (OF) | 1943–49 |
| Stubby Overmire (P) | 1943–49 |
| Frank Owen (P) | 1901 |
| Marv Owen (3B) | 1931, 1933–37 |
| Ray Oyler (SS) | 1965–68 |

## P

| | |
|---|---|
| John Pacella (P) | 1986 |
| Phil Page (P) | 1928–30 |
| David Palmer (P) | 1989 |
| Dean Palmer (3B) | 1999–2003 |
| Jose Paniagua (P) | 2002 |
| Stan Papi (3B) | 1980–81 |
| Craig Paquette (3B) | 2002–03 |
| John Paredes (2B) | 1990–91 |
| Mark Parent (C) | 1996 |
| Clay Parker (P) | 1990 |
| Salty Parker (SS) | 1936 |
| Slicker Parks (P) | 1921 |
| Lance Parrish (C) | 1977–86 |
| Dixie Parsons (C) | 1939, 1942–43 |
| Steve Partenheimer (3B) | 1913 |
| Johnny Pasek (C) | 1933 |
| Larry Pashnick (P) | 1982–83 |
| Bob Patrick (OF) | 1941–42 |
| Danny Patterson (P) | 2000–04 |
| Daryl Patterson (P) | 1968–71 |
| Jarrod Patterson (3B) | 2001 |
| Fred Payne (C) | 1906–08 |
| Terry Pearson (P) | 2002 |
| Marv Peasley (P) | 1910 |
| Al Pedrique (SS) | 1989 |

# Detroit Tigers All-Time Roster

| | | | |
|---|---|---|---|
| Rudy Pemberton (OF) | 1995 | Placido Polanco (2B) | 2005–06 |
| Carlos Pena (1B) | 2002–05 | Luis Polonia (OF) | 1999–2000 |
| Orlando Pena (P) | 1965–67 | Jim Poole (P) | 2000 |
| Ramon Pena (P) | 1989 | J.W. Porter (C) | 1955–57 |
| Shannon Penn (2B) | 1995–96 | Lew Post (OF) | 1902 |
| Gene Pentz (P) | 1975 | Brian Powell (P) | 1998, 2002 |
| Pepper Peploski (3B) | 1913 | Ray Powell (OF) | 1913 |
| Don Pepper (1B) | 1966 | Ted Power (P) | 1988 |
| Troy Percival (P) | 2005 | Del Pratt (2B) | 1923–24 |
| Neifi Perez (2B) | 2006 | Joe Presko (P) | 1957–58 |
| Matt Perisho (P) | 2001–02 | Jim Price (C) | 1967–71 |
| Cy Perkins (PH) | 1934 | Jerry Priddy (2B) | 1950–53 |
| Hub Pernoll (P) | 1910, 1912 | Curtis Pride (OF) | 1996–97 |
| Ron Perranoski (P) | 1971–72 | Jim Proctor (P) | 1959 |
| Pol Perritt (P) | 1921–22 | Augie Prudhomme (P) | 1929 |
| Boyd Perry (SS) | 1941 | Tim Pugh (P) | 1997 |
| Clay Perry (3B) | 1908 | Billy Purtell (3B) | 1914 |
| Hank Perry (OF) | 1912 | Ed Putman (C) | 1979 |
| Jim Perry (P) | 1973 | | |
| Johnny Pesky (2B) | 1952–54 | **Q** | |
| John Peters (C) | 1915 | George Quellich (OF) | 1931 |
| Rick Peters (OF) | 1979–81 | | |
| Ben Petrick (OF) | 2003 | **R** | |
| Dan Petry (P) | 1979–87, 1990–91 | Mike Rabel (C) | 2006 |
| Gary Pettis (OF) | 1988–89, 1992 | Ryan Raburn (2B) | 2004 |
| Adam Pettyjohn (P) | 2001 | Dick Radatz (P) | 1969 |
| Dave Philley (OF) | 1957 | Rip Radcliff (OF) | 1941–43 |
| Bubba Phillips (3B) | 1955, 1963–64 | Ed Rakow (P) | 1964–65 |
| Eddie Phillips (C) | 1929 | Joe Randa (3B) | 1998 |
| Jack Phillips (1B) | 1955–57 | Earl Rapp (OF) | 1949 |
| Red Phillips (P) | 1934, 1936 | Jim Ray (P) | 1974 |
| Tony Phillips (OF) | 1990–95 | Bugs Raymond (P) | 1904 |
| Billy Pierce (P) | 1945, 1948 | Mark Redman (P) | 2001–02 |
| Jack Pierce (1B) | 1975 | Wayne Redmond (OF) | 1965, 1969 |
| Tony Piet (3B) | 1938 | Bob Reed (P) | 1969–70 |
| Herman Pillette (P) | 1922–24 | Jody Reed (2B) | 1997 |
| Luis Pineda (P) | 2001 | Rich Reese (1B) | 1973 |
| Babe Pinelli (3B) | 1920 | Phil Regan (P) | 1960–65 |
| Wally Pipp (1B) | 1913 | Frank Reiber (OF) | 1933–36 |
| Cotton Pippen (P) | 1939–40 | Alex Remneas (P) | 1912 |
| Chris Pittaro (3B) | 1985–86 | Erwin Renfer (P) | 1913 |
| Al Platte (OF) | 1913 | Tony Rensa (C) | 1930 |
| Johnny Podres (P) | 1966–67 | Bob Reynolds (P) | 1975 |
| Boots Poffenberger (P) | 1937–38 | Ross Reynolds (P) | 1914–15 |

161

| | | | |
|---|---|---|---|
| Billy Rhiel (3B) | 1932–33 | Dave Rozema (P) | 1977–84 |
| Dennis Ribant (P) | 1968 | Art Ruble (OF) | 1927 |
| Harry Rice (OF) | 1928–30 | Dave Rucker (P) | 1981–83 |
| Paul Richards (C) | 1943–46 | Muddy Ruel (C) | 1931–32 |
| Nolen Richardson (3B) | 1929, 1931–32 | Vern Ruhle (P) | 1974–77 |
| Rob Richie (OF) | 1989 | Sean Runyan (P) | 1998–2000 |
| Hank Riebe (C) | 1942, 1947–49 | Jack Russell (P) | 1937 |
| Topper Rigney (SS) | 1922–25 | | |
| Bill Ripken (2B) | 1998 | **S** | |
| Kevin Ritz (P) | 1989–92 | Erik Sabel (P) | 2002 |
| Mike Rivera (C) | 2001–02 | A.J. Sager (P) | 1996–98 |
| Mike Roarke (C) | 1961–64 | Mark Salas (C) | 1990–91 |
| Bruce Robbins (P) | 1979–80 | Luis Salazar (OF) | 1988 |
| Bip Roberts (OF) | 1998 | Oscar Salazar (SS) | 2002 |
| Dave Roberts (P) | 1976–77 | Ron Samford (SS) | 1955, 1957 |
| Leon Roberts (OF) | 1974–75 | Juan Samuel (2B) | 1994–95 |
| Willis Roberts (P) | 1999 | Joe Samuels (P) | 1930 |
| Jerry Robertson (P) | 1970 | Alejandro Sanchez (OF) | 1985 |
| Nate Robertson (P) | 2003–06 | Alex Sanchez (OF) | 2003–04 |
| Aaron Robinson (C) | 1949–51 | Reggie Sanders (1B) | 1974 |
| Eddie Robinson (1B) | 1957 | Scott Sanders (P) | 1997–98 |
| Jeff Robinson (P) | 1987–90 | Julio Santana (P) | 2002 |
| Rabbit Robinson (3B) | 1904 | Marino Santana (P) | 1998 |
| Fernando Rodney (P) | 2002–06 | Pedro Santana (2B) | 2001 |
| Aurelio Rodriguez (3B) | 1971–79 | Ramon Santiago (SS) | 2002–03, 2006 |
| Ivan Rodriguez (C) | 2004–06 | Victor Santos (P) | 2001 |
| Steve Rodriguez (2B) | 1995 | Joe Sargent (2B) | 1921 |
| Joe Rogalski (P) | 1938 | Kevin Saucier (P) | 1981–82 |
| Billy Rogell (SS) | 1930–39 | Dennis Saunders (P) | 1970 |
| Kenny Rogers (P) | 2006 | Bob Scanlan (P) | 1996 |
| Saul Rogovin (P) | 1949–51 | Ray Scarborough (P) | 1953 |
| Mel Rojas (P) | 1999 | Germany Schaefer (2B) | 1905–09 |
| Bill Roman (1B) | 1964–65 | Biff Schaller (OF) | 1911 |
| Ed Romero (3B) | 1990 | Wally Schang (C) | 1931 |
| Henri Rondeau (C) | 1913 | Dan Schatzeder (P) | 1980–81 |
| Matt Roney (P) | 2003 | Frank Scheibeck (2B) | 1906 |
| Jim Rooker (P) | 1968 | Fred Scherman (P) | 1969–73 |
| Cody Ross (OF) | 2003 | Bill Scherrer (P) | 1984–86 |
| Don Ross (OF) | 1938, 1942–45 | Lou Shiappacasse (OF) | 1902 |
| Claude Rossman (1B) | 1907–09 | Brian Schmack (P) | 2003 |
| Larry Rothschild (P) | 1981–82 | Boss Schmidt (C) | 1906–11 |
| Jack Rowan (P) | 1906 | Rick Schu (3B) | 1989 |
| Schoolboy Rowe (P) | 1933–42 | Heinie Schuble (SS) | 1929, 1932–35 |
| Rich Rowland (C) | 1990–93 | Barney Schultz (P) | 1959 |

| | | | |
|---|---:|---|---:|
| Bob Schultz (P) | 1955 | Bob Smith (P) | 1959 |
| Mike Schwabe (P) | 1989–90 | Clay Smith (P) | 1940 |
| Chuck Scrivener (SS) | 1975–77 | George C. Smith (2B) | 1963–65 |
| Johnny Seale (P) | 1964–65 | George S. Smith (P) | 1926–29 |
| Steve Searcy (P) | 1988–91 | Heinie Smith (2B) | 1903 |
| Tom Seats (P) | 1940 | Jack Smith (3B) | 1912 |
| Bobby Seay (P) | 2006 | Jason Smith (SS) | 2002–03 |
| Frank Secory (OF) | 1940 | Rufus Smith (P) | 1927 |
| Chuck Seelbach (P) | 1971–74 | Willie Smith (P) | 1963 |
| Ray Semproch (P) | 1960 | Nate Snell (P) | 1987 |
| Rip Sewell (P) | 1932 | Clint Sodowsky (P) | 1995–96 |
| Dick Sharon (OF) | 1973–74 | Vic Sorrell (P) | 1928–37 |
| Al Shaw (C) | 1901 | Elias Sosa (P) | 1982 |
| Bob Shaw (P) | 1957–58 | Steve Souchock (OF) | 1951–55 |
| Merv Shea (C) | 1927–29, 1939 | Steve Sparks (P) | 2000–03 |
| Larry Sheets (OF) | 1990 | Joe Sparma (P) | 1964–69 |
| John Shelby (OF) | 1990–91 | Kid Speer (P) | 1909 |
| Hugh Shelley (OF) | 1935 | George Spencer (P) | 1958, 1960 |
| Chris Shelton (1B) | 2004–06 | Tubby Spencer (C) | 1916–18 |
| Pat Sheridan (OF) | 1986–88 | Charlie Spikes (OF) | 1978 |
| Larry Sherry (P) | 1964–67 | Harry Spilman (3B) | 1986 |
| Jimmy Shevlin (1B) | 1930 | Chris Spurling (P) | 2003–06 |
| Ivey Shiver (OF) | 1931 | Tuck Stainback (OF) | 1940–41 |
| Ron Shoop (C) | 1959 | Matt Stairs (DH) | 2006 |
| Chick Shorten (OF) | 1919–21 | Gerry Staley (P) | 1961 |
| Joe Siddall (C) | 1998 | Oscar Stanage (C) | 1909–20, 1925 |
| Ruben Sierra (OF) | 1996 | Mickey Stanley (OF) | 1964–78 |
| Ed Siever (P) | 1901–02, 1906–08 | Joe Staton (1B) | 1972–73 |
| Frank Sigafoos (3B) | 1929 | Rusty Staub (OF) | 1976–79 |
| Al Simmons (OF) | 1936 | Bill Steen (P) | 1915 |
| Hack Simmons (1B) | 1910 | Dave Stegman (OF) | 1978–80 |
| Nelson Simmons (OF) | 1984–85 | Ben Steiner (P)inch runner | 1947 |
| Randall Simon (1B) | 2001–02 | Todd Steverson (OF) | 1995 |
| Duke Sims (C) | 1972–73 | Walter Stewart (P) | 1921 |
| Matt Sinatro (C) | 1989 | Phil Stidham (P) | 1994 |
| Duane Singleton (OF) | 1996 | Bob Stoddard (P) | 1985 |
| Dave Sisler (P) | 1959–60 | John Stone (OF) | 1928–33 |
| Dave Skeels (P) | 1910 | Lil Stoner (P) | 1922, 1924–29 |
| Lou Skizas (OF) | 1958 | Jesse Stovall (P) | 1904 |
| John Skopec (P) | 1903 | Mike Strahler (P) | 1973 |
| Jim Slaton (P) | 1978, 1986 | Bob Strampe (P) | 1972 |
| Bill Slayback (P) | 1972–74 | Doug Strange (3B) | 1989 |
| Lou Sleater (P) | 1957–58 | Walt Streuli (C) | 1954–56 |
| Jim Small (OF) | 1955–57 | Sailor Stroud (P) | 1910 |

| | | | |
|---|---|---|---|
| Marlin Stuart (P) | 1949–52 | Jason Thompson (1B) | 1976–80 |
| Franklin Stubbs (1B) | 1995 | Justin Thompson (P) | 1996–99 |
| Jim Stump (P) | 1957, 1959 | Sam Thompson (OF) | 1906 |
| Tom Sturdivant (P) | 1963 | Tim Thompson (C) | 1958 |
| Joe Sugden (1B) | 1912 | Gary Thurman (OF) | 1993 |
| George Suggs (P) | 1908–09 | Mark Thurmond (P) | 1986–87 |
| Billy Sullivan Jr. (C) | 1940–41 | Tom Timmerman (P) | 1968–73 |
| Billy Sullivan Sr. (C) | 1916 | Ron Tingley (C) | 1995 |
| Charlie Sullivan (P) | 1928, 1930–31 | Dave Tobik (P) | 1978–82 |
| Jack Sullivan (2B) | 1944 | Jim Tobin (P) | 1945 |
| Joe Sullivan (P) | 1935–36 | Kevin Tolar (P) | 2000–01 |
| John E. Sullivan (C) | 1905 | Tim Tolman (OF) | 1986–87 |
| John P. Sullivan (C) | 1963–65 | Andy Tomberlin (OF) | 1998 |
| Russ Sullivan (OF) | 1951–53 | Earl Torgeson (1B) | 1955–57 |
| Champ Summers (OF) | 1979–81 | Andres Torres (OF) | 2002–04 |
| Ed Summers (P) | 1908–12 | Dick Tracewski (SS) | 1966–69 |
| George C. Susce (C) | 1932 | Alan Trammell (SS) | 1977–96 |
| George D. Susce (P) | 1958–59 | Bubba Trammell (OF) | 1997 |
| Gary Sutherland (2B) | 1974–76 | Al Travers (P) | 1912 |
| Suds Sutherland (P) | 1921 | Tom Tresh (SS) | 1969 |
| Bill Sweeney (1B) | 1928 | Gus Triandos (C) | 1963 |
| Bob Swift (C) | 1944–53 | Dizzy Trout (P) | 1939–52 |
| Bob Sykes (P) | 1977–78 | Bun Troy (P) | 1912 |
| Ken Szotkiewicz (SS) | 1970 | Chris Truby (SS) | 2002 |
| | | Virgil Trucks (P) | 1941–43, 1945–52, 1956 |
| **T** | | Mike Trujillo (P) | 1988–89 |
| Frank Tanana (P) | 1985–92 | John Tsitouris (P) | 1957 |
| Jordan Tata (P) | 2006 | Jerry Turner (OF) | 1982 |
| Jackie Tavener (SS) | 1921, 1925–28 | Bill Tuttle (OF) | 1952, 1954–57 |
| Ben Taylor (1B) | 1952 | Guy Tutwiler (1B) | 1911, 1913 |
| Bill Taylor (OF) | 1957–58 | | |
| Bruce Taylor (P) | 1977–79 | **U** | |
| Gary Taylor (P) | 1969 | Bob Uhl (P) | 1940 |
| Tony Taylor (2B) | 1971–73 | George Uhle (P) | 1929–33 |
| Wiley Taylor (P) | 1911 | Jerry Ujdur (P) | 1980–83 |
| Birdie Tebbetts (C) | 1936–42, 1946–47 | Pat Underwood (P) | 1979–80, 1982–83 |
| Walt Terrell (P) | 1985–88, 1990–92 | Al Unser (C) | 1942–44 |
| John Terry (P) | 1902 | Tom Urbani (P) | 1996 |
| Mickey Tettleton (C) | 1991–94 | Ugueth Urbina (P) | 2004–05 |
| Marcus Thames (OF) | 2004–06 | Lino Urdaneta (P) | 2004 |
| Bud Thomas (P) | 1939–41 | | |
| Frosty Thomas (P) | 1905 | **V** | |
| George Thomas (OF) | 1957–58, 1961, 1964–65 | Vito Valentinetti (P) | 1958 |
| Ira Thomas (C) | 1908 | Elam Vangilder (P) | 1928–29 |

| | | | |
|---|---|---|---|
| Andy Van Hekken (P) | 2002 | Skeeter Webb (SS) | 1945–46 |
| Todd Van Poppel (P) | 1996 | Herm Wehmeier (P) | 1958 |
| Bobby Veach (OF) | 1912–23 | Dick Weik (P) | 1953–54 |
| Coot Veal (SS) | 1958–60, 1963 | Milt Welch (C) | 1945 |
| Lou Vedder (P) | 1920 | David Wells (P) | 1993–95 |
| Randy Veres (P) | 1996 | Ed Wells (P) | 1923–27 |
| Justin Verlander (P) | 2005–06 | Don Wert (3B) | 1963–70 |
| Tom Veryzer (SS) | 1973–77 | Vic Wertz (OF) | 1947–52, 1961–63 |
| George Vico (1B) | 1948–49 | Charlie Wheatley (P) | 1912 |
| Brandon Villafuerte (P) | 2000 | Jack Whillock (P) | 1971 |
| Fernando Vina (2B) | 2004 | Lou Whitaker (2B) | 1977–95 |
| Ozzie Virgil (3B) | 1958, 1960–61 | Derrick White (OF) | 1995 |
| Ossie Vitt (3B) | 1912–18 | Hal White (P) | 1941–43, 46–52 |
| | | Jo-Jo White (OF) | 1932–38 |
| **W** | | Rondell White (OF) | 2004–05 |
| Jake Wade (P) | 1936–38 | Earl Whitehill (P) | 1923–32 |
| Hal Wagner (C) | 1947–48 | Sean Whiteside (P) | 1995 |
| Mark Wagner (SS) | 1976–80 | Kevin Wickander (P) | 1995 |
| Dick Wakefield (OF) | 1941, 1943–44, 1946–49 | Dave Wickersham (P) | 1964–67 |
| Chris Wakeland (OF) | 2001 | Jimmy Wiggs (P) | 1905–06 |
| Matt Walbeck (C) | 1997, 2002–03 | Bill Wight (P) | 1952–53 |
| Jim Walewander (2B) | 1987–88 | Milt Wilcox (P) | 1977–85 |
| Dixie Walker (OF) | 1938–39 | Ed Willett (P) | 1906–13 |
| Frank Walker (OF) | 1917–18 | Brian Williams (P) | 1996 |
| Gee Walker (OF) | 1931–37 | Eddie Williams (OF) | 1996 |
| Hub Walker (OF) | 1931, 1935, 1945 | Frank Williams (P) | 1989 |
| Jamie Walker (P) | 2002–06 | Johnny Williams (P) | 1914 |
| Luke Walker (P) | 1974 | Ken Williams (OF) | 1989–90 |
| Mike Walker (P) | 1996 | Lefty Williams (P) | 1913–14 |
| Tom Walker (P) | 1975 | Carl Willis (P) | 1984 |
| Jim E. Walkup (P) | 1939 | Earl Wilson (P) | 1966–70 |
| Jim H. Walkup (P) | 1927 | Glenn Wilson (OF) | 1982–83 |
| Jim Walsh (P) | 1921 | Icehouse Wilson (PH) | 1934 |
| Steve Wapnik (P) | 1990 | Jack Wilson (P) | 1942 |
| Gary Ward (OF) | 1989–90 | Mutt Wilson (C) | 1920 |
| Hap Ward (OF) | 1912 | Red Wilson (C) | 1954–60 |
| Jon Warden (P) | 1968 | Squanto Wilson (C) | 1911 |
| Jack Warner (3B) | 1925–28 | Vance Wilson (C) | 2005–06 |
| John Warner (C) | 1905–06 | Walter Wilson (P) | 1945 |
| Johnny Watson (SS) | 1930 | Red Wingo (OF) | 1924–28 |
| Jeff Weaver (P) | 1999–2002 | George Winter (P) | 1908 |
| Jim Weaver (OF) | 1985 | Casey Wise (2B) | 1960 |
| Roger Weaver (P) | 1980 | Hugh Wise (C) | 1930 |
| Earl Webb (OF) | 1932–33 | Kevin Witt (1B) | 2003 |

| John Wockenfuss (C) | 1974–83 |
| Pete Wojey (P) | 1956–57 |
| Bob Wood (C) | 1904–05 |
| Jake Wood (2B) | 1961–67 |
| Jason Wood (1B) | 1998–99 |
| Joe Wood (2B) | 1943 |
| Larry Woodall (C) | 1920–29 |
| Hal Woodeshick (P) | 1956, 1961 |
| Ron Woods (OF) | 1969 |
| Mark Woodyard (P) | 2005 |
| Ralph Works (P) | 1909–12 |
| Tim Worrell (P) | 1998 |
| Yats Wuestling (SS) | 1929–30 |
| John Wyatt (P) | 1968 |
| Whit Wyatt (P) | 1929–33 |

**Y**

| Esteban Yan (P) | 2004 |
| Emil Yde (P) | 1929 |

| Joe Yeager (P/3B) | 1901–03 |
| Archie Yelle (C) | 1917–19 |
| Tom Yewcic (C) | 1957 |
| Rudy York (1B) | 1934, 1937–45 |
| Eddie Yost (3B) | 1959–60 |
| Dmitri Young (1B) | 2002–06 |
| Ernie Young (OF) | 2003 |
| John Young (1B) | 1971 |
| Kip Young (P) | 1978–79 |
| Ralph Young (2B) | 1915–21 |

**Z**

| Chris Zachary (P) | 1972 |
| Carl Zamloch (P) | 1913 |
| Bill Zepp (P) | 1971 |
| Gus Zernial (OF) | 1958–59 |
| Joel Zumaya (P) | 2006 |
| George Zuverink (P) | 1954–55 |

# Notes

### Wahoo Sam
"That's when I started touring…" Ritter, Lawrence S., *The Glory of Their Times*, New York: Macmillan Co., 1966.

### Along Came Cobb
"Stretched a double into a triple…" Ritter, Lawrence S., *The Glory of Their Times*, New York: Macmillan Co., 1966.

### Eee-Yah
"We do all right in the World Series until…" Bak, Richard, *Ty Cobb*, Dallas: Taylor Publishing, 1994.

### Old Slug
"I hit .334 for the Senators…" Ritter, Lawrence S., *The Glory of Their Times*, New York: Macmillan Co., 1966.

### The Silent Man
"Well, that did it." Honig, Donald, *Baseball When the Grass Was Real*, Lincoln, NE: University of Nebraska Press, 1975.

### Hammerin' Hank
"The national press had come out…" Honig, Donald, *Baseball When the Grass Was Real*, Lincoln, NE: University of Nebraska Press, 1975.

"For years after that…" Honig, Donald, *Baseball When the Grass Was Real*, Lincoln, NE: University of Nebraska Press, 1975.

## Bobo the Great

"Everybody was 'Bobo' to him..." Greenberg, Hank, with Ira Berkow, *Hank Greenberg: The Story of My Life*, Chicago: Triumph Books, 2000.

"He was overpowering in that one season..." Greenberg, Hank, with Ira Berkow, *Hank Greenberg: The Story of My Life*, Chicago: Triumph Books, 2000.

## The Kid from Baltimore

"The Yankees were so good..." Cantor, George, *Baseball's Last Real Champions*, Dallas: Taylor Publishing, 1997.

## 1984 and *The Natural*

"All I knew is that we were making history..." Cantor, George, *Wire to Wire*, Chicago: Triumph Books, 2004.

"I was in town that winter..." Cantor, George, *Wire to Wire*, Chicago: Triumph Books, 2004.